10.3

STRUGGLES OF
WOMEN
AT WORK

STRUGGLES OF
WOMEN
AT WORK

Edited by
Sujata Gothoskar

Under the auspices of
Indian Association for Women's Studies

VIKAS PUBLISHING HOUSE PVT LTD

VIKAS PUBLISHING HOUSE PVT LTD

576 Masjid Road, Jangpura, New Delhi 110 014 Ph. 4615313,4615570
Email: chawlap @ giasdl01.vsnl.net.in, Fax: 91-11-3276593

First Floor, N.S. Bhawan, 4th Cross, 4th Main,
Gandhi Nagar, Bangalore 560009 Ph. 2204639

Distributors:

UBS Publishers' Distributors Ltd

- 5, Ansari Road, **New Delhi**-110002 Ph. 3273601, 3266646
- Apeejay Chambers, 5 Wallace St., **Mumbai**-400001 Ph. 2070827, 2076971
- 10, First Main Road, Gandhi Nagar, **Bangalore**-560009 Ph. 2263901
- 6, Sivaganga Road, Nungambakkam, **Chennai**-600034 Ph. 8276355
- 8/1-B, Chowringhee Lane, **Calcutta**-700016 Ph. 2441821, 2442910
- 5-A, Rajendra Nagar, **Patna**- 800016 Ph. 652856, 656169
- 80, Noronha Road, Cantonment, **Kanpur**-208004 Ph. 369124, 362665

First Paperback Edition, 1997

Printed at Kay Kay Printers, Delhi-110007

Contents

Acknowledgements

I am grateful to the various people who have helped to put this book together. Over the years, the Forum Against Oppression of Women, the Union Research Group and the Workers' Solidarity Centre have helped me to continuously clarify my ideas and dare to dream. They made me more aware of how little we know and how much there is to learn. Trade Unionists and women workers in Bombay involved me in their movement and have contributed enormously to the information and the ideas I express here. The individual contributors to the collection have also taught me a great deal.

My friends, especially Vijay Kanhere, Suhas Paranjape, Nandita Gandhi, Rajesh Walawalkar, Swatija Manorama, Nandita Shah and Sandhya Gokhale have also helped me enormously by giving their suggestions and comments, in the editorial work as well as in putting the volume together. I sincerely thank all of them.

I would also like to thank Susheela Kaushik and the Indian Association for Women's Studies.

Sujata Gothoskar

General Introduction

For both academics of different disciplines and activists of diverse political and ideological positions in India, women's studies presents a compelling challenge to pause, take stock and amend their ways. Studies have continued and extended the awareness of the deprivations and discriminations which had been suffered by women and which had been reported earlier by the Committee on the Status of Women in India (1975). The two main findings of the Committee were that, more than in most countries of the world, gender based deprivation in India threatened not only women's quality of life, but even their chances of survival; and that these deprivations had been aggravated through a century of socio-economic development. The basic tone of Women's Studies in India having been set by these findings, Women's Studies in India. It became a continuous crusade in the cause of women, manifesting deep concern and anger at the existing situation and a strong commitment to sensitise the community to bring about needed social change.

The combined effect of the CSWI's Report and the International Women's Decade set off a chain of efforts-by research scholars, governmental agencies and others-to understand and analyse the conditions of women, to trace its origins and manifestations, and to grapple with remedial measures. These efforts were strengthened and greatly influenced by the debate on the women's question in the wider women's movement that erupted by 1977. Extensive research with innovative methodologies, brought new data on women's problems and roles, making the 'invisible' 'visible'. Analysis of their unequal status, lack of basic human rights and subjection to a wide variety of atrocities and abuses led to a sharpening of the debate and inspired greater awareness and more systematic research on women's issues. This qualitative shift in outlook and heightened consciousness distinguish the contemporary women's movement in India from its earlier forms. The emerging discipline of Women's Studies reflect this new consciousness and ideology.

Historically women's issues had been a major ingredient of social reform movement in modern India. Abolition of 'sati', and campaigns for widow remarriage, women's education, property rights and political rights were some of their focal points. The special needs of women workers in organised industry, and women's spontaneous role in the freedom struggle received some attention. However, all the earlier movements and their leaders had, by and large, accepted the existing pattern of gender relations, along with the division of labour and authority between men and women, as natural. The contemporary women's movement goes beyond concessions and benefits; it supports women's rights to equality, participation and role in decision making. The needed instrument for this is empowerment and not welfare.

It seeks to make every woman aware of the fact that her own relations with other members of her family or in the work place are not just a personal or private matter; to a significant extent they are political relations determined by the gender based hierarchy prevailing in the society.

The critical view has extended to a redefinition of education. Instead of viewing education as a primary tool to ensure women's development and social development, the whole educational process is being re-examined. The content of research and teaching, their assumptions, approach and methodology are being questioned, as responsible for the 'invisibility' of women's problems and their social inequality. The CSWI Report had asked the educational system to move for "a deliberate, planned and sustained effort so that the new values of equality of the sexes can replace the traditional value system of inequality". To achieve this, educational institutions and their processes need to be informed and adopt the concerns, values and the findings of women's studies.

Women's Studies has accumulated a body of knowledge which is not merely part of social science or a separate discipline, but one that, with its given values and commitment, seeks to correct imbalances and evolve a new social ethos and consciousness. It embodies the concern for women's equality and development. seeks explanations for women's social status in the historical evolution of society and attempts to counter the structures and forces of subordination through various ways. The UNESCO Meeting of Experts on Women's Studies and Social Sciences in Asia held in New Delhi in October 1982, defined Women's Studies in terms of the objectives that such studies sought to achieve, viz:

1. "To promote better and balanced understanding of our societies and how they are responding to the process of change;
2. To contribute to the pursuit of human rights;
3. To assist both men and women in understanding, recognising, and giving due importance to the roles actually played by women and men;
4. To investigate the causes of disparity, analysing structural factors in addition to attitudinal and cultural factors;
5. To empower women in their struggle for equality and for an effective presence in all areas of society and development;
6. To render 'invisible' women 'visible' and in particular the women of the most underprivileged strata".[1]

This definition was further developed by a group of Indian scholars as follows:

"The pursuit of a more comprehensive, critical and balanced understanding of social reality, whose essential components should include (i) Women's contribution to the social process; (ii) women's perception of their own lives, the broader social reality and their struggles and aspirations; (iii) roots and structures of inequality that lead to marginalisation, invisibility and exclusion of women from the scope, approaches and conceptual frameworks of most intellectual enquiry and social action".

The same group also elaborated the objectives, earlier defined at the UNESCO meeting as (i) to conscientise both men and women by helping them to understand, recognise and acknowledge the multi-dimensional roles played by women in society; (ii) to promote better understanding of the process of social, technological and environmental change; (iii) to contribute to the pursuit of human rights; (iv) to investigate the causes of gender disparity-analysing structural, cultural and attitudinal factors; (v) to empower women in their struggle against inequality; and for effective participation in all areas of society and development; (vi) to render 'invisible' women 'visible' in particular women of the underprivileged strata; and (vii) to help develop alternative concepts, approaches and strategies for development.[2]

Women's Studies, like some other recently emerging areas of social knowledge is a study from below. It does not merely seek information about a depressed section of the society, but also attempts to look at the social process from the perspective of that depressed group. Such a perspective does not merely help to widen the knowledge base regarding the social process or promote new methods of enquiry and concepts in the academic sphere. It may also alter society's dominant perceptions, and set in motion new policy approaches. Above all, adoption of the perspectives of groups even more subordinated and powerless than themselves transforms the intellectual and emotional outlook of the researcher-of either sex.[3]

Defined thus, Women's Studies has a close relationship with, and needs to be an integral part of the academic system in teaching, research and extension activities. Unless the educational system internalises the concerns for gender equality, and the recognition of women's role in society, it cannot contribute positively to the realisation of human rights and a just and human social order. It may be forced to continue its present rudderless existence, to be used by reactionary forces which want a very different society.

Awareness of this link made a group of Indian academics concerned about the future and they welcome women's studies as a perspective that could help educational institutions;

1. To change the present attitudes/values in society regarding women's roles, and rights, to one of equal participation in all social, economic and political processes and national and international development;

2. To promote awareness among women and men, of the need to develop and utilise women's full potential as resources for national development in its economic, political and socio-cultural aspects, on the need to question existing values and of their social responsibility so as to participate equally;

3. To counter the reactionary forces emanating from certain sections of the media, economic, social and political institutions, that encourage the demotion of women from productive to mere reproductive roles;

4. To revitalise university education, bringing it closer to burning social issues, to work towards their solution, and to produce sensitive persons able to play more committed and

meaningful roles in development activities for women in all sectors;

5. To fulfil a special responsibility-to produce for all levels of the educational system, teachers who are aware of the need for a non-sexist education, and who would actively pick up the challenge, to promote values of social equality, including gender equality, secularism, socialism and democracy;

6. To update university curricula by incorporating the results of new scholarship and the issues raised by the latter, as they challenge some of the established theories, analytical concepts and methodologies of various disciplines;

7. To promote increased collaboration between different disciplines in teaching, curriculum designing, research and extension activities since Women's Studies is interdisciplinary in nature;

8. To generate new and organic knowledge through intensive field work. This would help in the generation of data essential for evaluation and correction of development policies and programmes and in extending the areas for academic analysis into hitherto neglected sectors for a better understanding and investigation of problems being experienced by women at the grass-roots, closer contact between institutions of higher education and groups directly involved in action to assist women to enjoy their rights within the family, the community and at work, will be very valuable and help universities and colleges to design their extension activities in a more meaningful manner;

9. To contribute to the global debate on the women's question through rediscovery of the debate in India-from ancient to contemporary periods, through research and translation from Indian literature including folk literature.[4]

This critical connection between academic exercise and action gives women's studies its dynamism. As an academic study, it enriches the discipline and provides entirely new perspectives to analyse situations. It has a dual role as a discourse and a movement and provides contextualisation of knowledge in the process of both understanding and changing women's reality. As a movement it emphasises the need for providing legitimacy and material basis for women's equality, independence and empowerment. It is the live contact with the real situation which provides insights into the dynamics of social processes which is not normally possible from 'distant' academia.

Academic acceptance or understanding of this role and nature of women's studies is still neither widespread, nor uniform, though the movement has won some outstanding allies during its decade long struggle. The First National Conference on Women's Studies at Bombay (1981) sought to extend research activities which were confined to individuals, to a general challenge to the educational system. The Conference also gave birth to the Indian Association for Women's Studies, to carry on the struggle, through the joint forum of academics and activists.

The national conferences, regional conferences and workshops organised by the Association has helped to influence the spread and development of Women's Studies in a way different from other academic disciplines, by emphasising this extra dimension. Most researchers get drawn into activism in the course of their work. They develop a sense of personal involvement and a sense of participation in the women's movement and in the lives of women whom they are studying. At the same time, a large number of activists feel the need to understand the background of the discrimination against women; to synthesise and systematise the information they collect and to analyse it with a view to bring out the basic patterns of oppression.

Tensions, however, are inevitable in balancing the search for quality and rigour in theory and practice, with mobilisation for the movement; between autonomy for untramelled growth and a catalyst role to influence the wider systems; between the compulsion to adopt and use feminist terminology which restricts communication to the converted and the informed few, and a language commonly understood by many. There is a need to build bridges between the highly educated and women at the grassroots - very often illiterate - whose perspectives, priorities and participation are essential to the movement.

Women's studies in India can rightfully boast of many achievements. An impressive corpus of research generated over the past few years has been devoted to finding and collating factual information about various aspects of gender based inequalities in different classes, castes, communities and cultures; identifying some of the most significant structures and instruments of subordination in their contemporary and historic forms.

Standard concepts, models and definitions used by conventional academic disciplines have been challenged successfully with valid data.

A major example is the concept of work and workers, work participation rates and productive work as defined in Economics and by Census and other data collecting agencies. Measured in terms of market orientation, the whole gamut of activities in the household economy - directly or indirectly contributing to the income, savings and maintenance of the households, had been ignored in computing work.

The other side of these complex relationship are people's struggles against oppression and inequality. Investigating women in such struggles - present or past, evolving concepts of power-personal or political - are some of the other areas where Women's Studies has made new inroads and challenged the existing methods of examining source materials and gender based interpretations. Thus, whether in history, culture or literacy analysis, Women's Studies is seeking to recast social science analysis from an entirely different set of values and perspectives. An exciting mixture of concepts and methodologies drawn from several disciplines, combined with the use of various non-traditional source materials, has created a rich resource for reanalysis of social structures, artefacts and hierarchies. They have, also helped to demystify the nature of gender relations. In the process, women's studies has successfully combated the notions of women as the 'weaker' sex needing protection, challenged concepts of women's 'upliftment' 'backwardness' and sought to replace social service for women's welfare by developmental research and action so as to achieve women's empowerment for participation and partnership.

The initial preoccupation of women's studies in obtaining recognition for women's labour concentrated a large part of the research effort in this sector - extending immediately to examining macro-economic processes from the perspective of women becoming marginalised by such processes. The informal sector in both urban and rural areas where women were concentrated was the next to receive attention, identifying thereby new questions for investigation.

From the household as an economic unit to the household as a political unit - where power relations, authority structures and resource allocations take place - was an inevitable transition. In investigating this, however, the complexity and diversity of Indian social organisations, the roles of caste, class, community and culture posed some serious difficulties. Complicating the situation further is the role of state policy and legislation, which contain many ambiguities and contradictions. Women's Studies had to grapple with issues of family legislation on the one hand and policies and measures affecting sectors like natural resource management, environmental degradation, inter sectoral transfer and regulation of resources, etc., on the other and the ever present balancing game between political supremacy and the compulsions of government also had to be confronted in order to demonstrate that all of them affected gender relations in society.

Such realities need to be brought close to people's understanding through the school/college system and be reflected in teaching content and methodologies. Integration within the general curriculum was a pragmatic decision voiced by participants in the First National Conference, who wanted Women's Studies to make an impact not merely on social awareness and value formation of the younger generation, but also on the educational system per se - to correct some of its present maladies. Hence, the struggle (often within the movement too) to maintain that Women's Studies is neither a discipline nor a subject which can be safely reflected to one academic subject and be marginalised. It is a dimension, perspective and an ideology that requires articulation in every discipline and faculty, in every institution and at every level. Incorporation of specific themes pertaining to women's question in a broader course, of women's dimension and perspectives in the general topics falling within the general and compulsory courses, and seeking to reach them to the widest range of scholars are some of the strategies of creating a social impact. Such an incorporation in turn, should be followed by emphasising the necessary supports like research, community action, library, documentation and information networking, fellowships, seminars, workshops, summer institutes etc., This stance has been based on the belief that teaching is a widespread and necessary 'action' that reaches out to the maximum number of persons, urban and rural, colleges and scholars, rich and poor, and above all men and women.

Such a curricullar development in turn involves

(a)   an examination of existing syllabi for their sex bias and perpetuation of stereotyped gender values that seek to make women's work and contribution invisible or devalued - thereby making women appear weak; soft, dependent, mere appendages to men and burdensome;

(b)   a revision of syllabi, and the structure, to make them reflect women's concerns more 'visibly' and coherently - not as an adjunct often contradictory to the main course; content.

(c)   a reoriented teaching methodology which would necessitate inter-disciplinary and inter-departmental interaction and approach;

(d)   new methodologies of teaching cum field action in the form of clinics, services, field surveys, action research, and field analysis of policies and programmes.

The need for a fusion of different approaches, specialisations, and areas of knowledge, in order to bring about a qualitative change in the established disciplines, have long been felt; Women's Studies seeks to achieve this.

Origin and Growth of I.A.W.S.

Following the resolution of the first National Conference on Women's Studies, held at the SNDT Women's University, Bombay 1981, the Indian Association for Women's Studies was formed in 1982 with the following objectives:

1.   To provide a forum for interaction amongst individuals, institutions and organisations engaged in teaching, research or action for women's development;

2.   To provide and establish information centres at different parts of the country for promotion of Women's Studies and scientific analysis of action for development promoting women's equality. To this end to develop a network for collection of information relating to teaching, research and action programmes;

    a.   to develop documentation, bibliographic and other services;

    b.   to disseminate needed information to all agencies engaged in teaching, research and action programmes.

3.   To organise periodical conferences to carry forward the awareness and momentum generated by the First National Conference which was organised by the SNDT Women's University, Bombay, Kanpur University and Centre for Women's Development Studies, New Delhi in April 1981;

4.   To organise specific action programmes for the development of Women's Studies Perspectives in different disciplines and for the development of appropriate indicators for measuring

women's participation in social and economic development;
5.   To mobilise necessary services and resources, with a view to strengthen and assist women scholars, writers and communicators to develop their talents;
6.   To assist institutions seeking to develop programmes for teaching, research and action for women's equality and development;
7.   To take all such action that may be deemed necessary, to bring about a change in social values with a view to eliminate attitudinal, conceptual and class biases that hinder understanding of the role and situation of women and their movement towards equality; and
8.   To collaborate with institutions and agencies working for similar objectives at the national and international level.

Since its inception the Association has organised four National Conferences in 1984 (Trivandrum), 1986 (Chandigarh), 1988 (Waltair) and 1991 (Calcutta). Each of these conferences focussed on a particular theme, adopting a modality of a series of workshops around sub-themes. In addition, each conference also had two or three special plenary sessions. In all these conferences, participants included representatives from neighbouring countries of South Asia.

In addition, the Association also organised an Asian Regional Conference on "Women and the Household", in collaboration with the Commission on Women of the IUAES and the Research Committee 32, on Women and Society, of the International Sociological Association. Participants included scholars and activists from various Asian countries, as well as a large number of Asian Studies specialists from Europe, United States, Latin America and Africa.

The Association also helped to organise a regional conference for Hindi speaking states at Kanpur in 1985, on "Women and Public Policy".

Besides the above conferences, the Association has undertaken, from time to time, organisation of task forces and small workshops on relatively neglected areas with a view to identifying needed action and research strategies. One such task force was appointed soon after the Trivandrum Conference on the basis of a resolution adopted there. It sought to promote research on the Role of Women in the Indian Freedom Struggle. The task force identified research strategies and approaches, bringing them to the attention of research funding agencies such as the I.C.H.R., I.C.S.S.R. and select Universities/scholars working on the freedom struggle. As a result, both the institutions have stepped up their support to research in this field and a renewed interest has been noted among doctoral students. In 1987, the Association appointed two task forces to examine the implications of the section titled "Education for Women's Equality" in the National Policy on Education, 1986. The first task force took up the issue of access to education for the large majority of women who are currently victims of lack of education or discrimination in access. Small diagnostic studies were undertaken in different parts of the country on different aspects of this major problem and a workshop was held in July 1987 to identify needed areas for intervention by educational institutions as well as by voluntary organisations committed to gender equality. The programmes of adult education, non-formal education and universalisation of elementary education, training/reorientation of teachers and the use of mass media being implemented by the Government of India were subjected to an extensive critique on the basis of the evaluative and diagnostic exercise undertaken by different members of the Task Force. Recommendations were formulated for the Government as well as for the members themselves, and were widely publicised through the press and electronic media.

The second Task Force examined the role of Science and Technology, particularly of institutions responsible for education in this field, in promoting gender equality. Since the previous workshop had identified discrimination in access to science education at the school level, the Task Force undertook some critical investigation in this issue in six selected states, and in the field of professional education in science based areas (e.g. agriculture, technology) at the University level. The findings of this investigation were presented and discussed at a national workshop on "Women, Science and Technology", hosted by the Indian Institute of Science, and sponsored by the Department of Science and Technology, Government of India, at Bangalore in November, 1988.

The exercise brought in, for the first time, a number of scientists - women and men - into the Association's field of activities. It has been a fruitful relationship, resulting in considerable sensitisation and concern among the senior scientists who participated in the workshop, through identification of structural and institutional biases which were found operative in women's access to education, training and employment in science based fields.

Such conferences apart from the interactions that they promote among participants, also throw up recommendations and resolutions.

These are utilised by the Association to organise policy dialogues and to bring pressure on the government. In 1985, the President of the Association, Dr. Madhuri R. Shah, wrote to the Education Minister stressing the need to incorporate women's studies within the educational system as an instrument to bring about changes in societal values and perspectives. In April 1985, the Association initiated with the U.G.C. a national workshop on the Organisation and Perspectives of Women's Studies in the Indian University System. In November 1985 the Ministry of Education convened a national seminar on Education for Women's Equality in which the Association was widely represented. Three months before the adoption by Parliament, of National Policy on Education, 1986, the UGC issued Guidelines for Development of Women's Studies in Universities, in the drafting of which Association members played a leading role. Since then the Association has taken considerable pains to mobilise faculty support within institutions to accelerate the implementation of women's studies.

As a result of its efforts, Women's Studies Centres/Cells have been established in nearly 50 University departments and colleges all over India. Research in Women's Studies has proliferated in higher education. As they do so, the close interaction between research and action, between theory and praxis, and between university and community, is emerging as a distinct feature of the Women's Studies movement in India. The Association by initiating steps in this direction and by providing space in the form of Conferences and Workshops, has contributed immensely.

Over the last ten years, the Association through its commitment and the work of its members, has been able to carve out a place for itself both within the Women's movement as and within academic centres concerned with educational reforms. Its national conferences have been well attended by men and women belonging to various walks of life. The Association has been recognised by the different departments of the government as well as the non-governmental agencies as the most successful mobilising body that can help identify educational institutions in different parts of the country who can effectively contribute to development programmes involving women as partners, as well as to identifying scholars which can take up research in needed areas. The University Grants Commission, Indian Council of Social Science Research and other agencies have established linkages with the Association by giving it representation on their Standing Committees.

Promotion of teaching being one of its major objectives the Association recognised from the beginning the need to bring packaged information based on the new scholarship within easy access of teachers and students. Considering the extent of work on Women's Studies in India, publications have been few in number and scattered creating difficulties for the new Women's Studies Centres and academic activists who are keen to redesign the curricula. The papers presented at various conferences and workshops represent a resource-as they cover many parts of the country. Selected papers of the Regional conference on "Women and the Household" were published in five volumes earlier. The present series of eleven volumes draw on the selected papers of the first four bienial National Conferences of the Association. Though some of the papers were written several years earlier, they do help to demonstrate the growth and development of women's studies in India through its period of infancy.

Publication of these volumes would have been impossible without the enormous efforts of their editors. The Association acknowledges, the contribution of the editors, authors and members of the Executive Committee in planning and implementing this mammoth project.

Chapter 1

Introduction

SUJATA GOTHOSKAR

M ost attempts at documenting struggles of women at work relate
to the few intense and glorious moments of organised struggle
that manage to get known to the world outside the immediate area
where they took place. However, these struggles often base themselves
on the day-to-day on going struggles of women, often alone and
sometimes in smaller or bigger groups. Without these unceasing
individual struggles, not only are collective struggles not possible, but
the very day-to-day survival and existence of women depends on these.

The most basic struggle of women revolves around trying to get
enough to eat for their families and for themselves and procuring the
most basic necessities of life such as food, water, fuel, fodder and shelter.
This struggle is made even more grim because as women they have
very little control over the conditions and products of their labour.
They have almost no say in deciding who gets how much of the family's
meagre resources.

For most men, even poor men, struggle does not take the same
implications as for women. For men, struggle is generally confined to
the work place, while home and leisure offer a contrast; whereas for
almost every woman, like her work, struggle too seems to occupy her
entire life. For women, there is no clear division in their work and
leisure, in paid and unpaid work, in work and non-work relations.
Personal, intimate relations for women are also work relations and
authority relations. But they are also personal-familial relations -
relations of caring and co-operation as well as of contradictions and

hostility, of emotions as well as subordination. Allies in one aspect of life are antagonists in another. Thus struggle itself may not always be a source of strength, but also of tensions, not merely of self-assertion, but also of self-effacement.

This renders struggle a complicated phenomenon in women's lives, without which not only survival, but also their elementary human dignity is at stake. Without struggle the fulfilment of the most simple aspirations of escaping a life of degradation and humiliation is threatened. Struggle often however does not make it any easier. These are the implications of struggle for millions of women in this country as in many others.

In the vast majority of cases, women's struggle remains an isolated one. This being the case, the odds are so heavily weighted against the lone woman that often after several attempts she despairs and sees no way out of her situation. Yet, the compulsions of survival and her aspirations for basic human dignity drive her on. What happens to women in this ever-conflictual situation they are in, depends on the individual situations of women, the support they receive from others of their kind and the balance of forces which are beyond their control and often against them. What in fact seems amazing is that despite these heavy odds, women continue to struggle - individually and collectively.

Often struggles of women at work are looked at or analysed from the point of view of their implications for social change. It is explicitly argued or implied that women's participation in collective struggles expresses their involvement in or commitment to the process of this change. Women's lack of participation, or the lack of visibility of women's struggles has often been equated with women's disinterest in the process of social change. The lack of visibility of women's struggles, even collective struggles, is related to a number of factors:

1.   Women are often more involved in the initial period of struggle, when struggles are intense and alterna organisations like unions or people's organisations have not yet stabilised. Once these acquire some stability, women are often sent back to the hearths, and men take over the stable organisations. It is often these stable organisations that are the subjects of study in academia and research.

2.   The majority of women, even in industrial production, work in the unorganised sectors. They participate in the struggles of these sectors. However, most struggles in these sectors

are not success stories, but stories of repeated defeats and failures, which are again not of interest to the same extent as success stories are.

3. Collective struggles are but one aspect of the struggles women are involved in, while for men these encompass their notion of struggle per se. As Louise Tilly points out, political history often ignores women (and men) who have no formal political roles. Thus, to remember that most women's political action has taken place outside the public sphere is to expand our definitions beyond the narrow terms of conventional wisdom.[1]

4. Besides, most researchers are upper class, upper caste persons (often men) and have their own very strong biases about women workers. These very strongly colour their perceptions of women workers and their struggles as Saswati Ghosh's article on jute workers in this volume documents.

Women's so-called disinterest in collective struggles has been a constant refrain of trade unions as well as political parties. Their censure of women has been somewhat less severe more recently as there has been some discussion on the entire issue of personal and political struggles, private and public spheres, and the connection between day-to-day struggles and revolutionary struggles.

Some problems with the forces and institutions that censure women for their so-called disinterest or non-involvement are: (1) their rigid framework of what constitutes social change and the process of social change, and (2) the consequent myopic vision which views women, their lives and struggles from the point of view of their own rigid framework. This rigid framework is hardly ever questioned. Nor is it reworked on in the light of the lives and struggles of women and other struggling sections of people.

According to Diane Elson, 'Women are experts at outwardly complying with authority, especially male authority, while inwardly rejecting its legitimacy. Women have had to learn to be patient, to bide their time, in their dealings with male authority in the home, so it is not surprising if this response is transferred to the factory. But the evidence from many studies suggests that when women workers are aroused to take militant action, they are tenacious in pursuit of their goal...As one male trade union official put it. "It is much harder to get the women out on strike than the men, but once they are out, it's muchharder to get them back in.'[2]

In this volume we will look at only issues related to struggles of women in their employment and in wage work, as the other aspects regarding other work and survival issues have been taken up in other volumes.

One limitation of this volume is that it includes a selection of only the papers written for or presented at either one of the first four conferences organised by the Indian Association for Women's Studies (IAWS). Many relevant accounts of struggles could not be included as full-length articles since they were not written for or presented at the conferences. I have tried to mention some of them in the following pages.

In this chapter I have tried to put forward the factors that determine the struggles of women as they have emerged in the different chapters of this volume and the forms of organisation women have experimented with.

Women's Employment Situation

The majority of women workers is concentrated in the unorganised sector, where the situation is pitted heavily against women workers and in favour of their employers. This is one reason why in most accounts of trade unions or workers' struggles, women get very little coverage.

Gradually, over the years, from the beginning of the century the proportion of women in the unorganised sector is increasing. In occupations or professions like teaching, finance and other service sector, especially what is called white-collar work, the employment of women has increased. "The service sector reflects the exact reverse of manufacturing industry, the largest concentration being in the public sector. It is in this sector that their employment has grown substantially. If 1974 is taken as the base, the increase by 1984 is of the order of 118.4 points in transport and communications and 167 points in financial services. In spite of this impressive growth, the gross numbers are quite meagre both in absolute terms as well as in relation to manufacturing. The implication may be that such avenues as exist for employment of women are increasingly for the middle classes with some education rather than for unskilled and semi-skilled women from the working class."[3]

In blue-collar employment there has been a systematic decline in woman's employment since the year 1920, once industry was beginning to stabilise. From 1920 to 1975, the proportion of women workers in textile, jute, and mining reduced from 20, 15 and 38 percent to 2.5, 2 and 5 percent, respectively.[4]

This decline in the employment and recruitment of women is not merely in the older industries like textiles, but disturbingly, also in the more modern industries, which only two or three decades ago employed a substantial number of women, such as the electronics, food and pharmaceutical industries, as discussed in the article in this volume on struggles by pharmaceutical women workers in Bombay by Sujata Gothoskar.

Reasons for the declining employment of women

Some of the underlying factors behind this discrimination against women in employment have been described as follows.

(1) *The idea of the 'family wage'* — the notion that a man should earn enough to feed his wife and children, while women should stay at home and do the unwaged work — housework, childcare, etc. Trade unions too have accepted this concept. Two union officials in Bengal who were interviewed by the Royal Commission on Factory Labour (1931) argued for a wage which would be sufficient to support female dependents as well as children. The All India Trade Union Congress too argued that in calculating the minimum wage, the standard working class family should be taken to comprise three consumption units for one earner, the earnings of women, children and adolescents being disregarded.[5]

In her article in this volume, Nivedita Menon has gone into how these notions have persisted where trade unions and union policies are concerned.

This attitude could possibly stem from two sources.

(i) Protest by trade unions against the extreme brutality and exploitation of men, women and children by the millowners. The millowners would have preferred to leave no time or space for the reproduction of the working capacity of their labour force, either from day to day or from generation to generation. By contrast, the union leaders recognised the need of children to be cared for and be educated, and acknowledged implicitly that running a household and caring for children was a full-time job for which someone had to be maintained.

(ii)   However, the unions assumed that women alone would do this work, while it would be paid through the man's wage. The unions uncritically accepted the age-old sexual division of labour and based their strategies on this acceptance. This assumption is not only erroneous but also detrimental to the interests of women and of the unions too. Eg., when jobs became scarce in the Indian textile industry in the 1930s, the Delhi Agreement was signed in 1935 by unions, the main terms of which were "that out of a family of two wage earners, women should be displaced".[6] The wage increase as a result of the new machines (for the men) was to be only 45 per cent, more than a 50 per cent loss of income for the family.

According to Diane Elson, the 'family wage' is an illusion. It is rare for a working man to earn enough to support wife and children at a decent standard. Women nearly always have to contribute some earning to the family budget. The 'family wage' for the men is more of a goal than a reality. It is a goal which has strong support in the organised labour movement in many countries, but an implication of this goal is that women should remain dependent on men.[7]

(2)   The assumption that women are solely responsible for running the home has been an important support for the introduction of *protective legislation*. Introduction of protective legislation has often been stated as an important reason for managements' preference for male workers and their discrimination against women in recruitment.

An important reason for the struggle for protective legislation like regulating the maximum working hours was the inhuman conditions of women workers and their children. Morbidity and mortality among women and especially children was very high and increasing.[8]

In Bombay the major reason for the reduction of women workers in the cotton textile industry was the restriction on night work. From the 1920s onwards a process of rationalisation took place and by 1930 most mills were running a night shift. Knowing that they had no possible alternative source of employment in the organised sector, women opposed the attempts of millowners to retrench them, arguing instead that they should share whatever work was available. Thus there was no catastrophic decline in their numbers but recruitment virtually stopped and there was a gradual reduction in the number of women, as is discussed in Radha Kumar's article in this volume. The same seems to be true of women workers in the pharmaceutical industry especially in terms of the lack of promotional avenues as well as recruitment.

(3)   Related to both the above factors is the idea of *industry as the main preserve of men*. Within industrial employment as also in other wage-work, there is the segregation of men and women into different types of jobs - for example, the preponderance of women in jobs like packing and assembling while engineering jobs are monopolised by men. This division partially overlaps with another one - the division into low-paid and well-paid jobs. This upto some extent precludes any 'competition' between women and men. The notion of industry as the main domain of men seems to have become a structural factor right from its inception and continues to this day.[9]

In fact, a dual process seems to have occurred. Jobs involving a higher degree of education, training and skill are both more prestigious and hence also better-paid. Women seem to be more or less completely excluded from these because they have less access to education and training. The consequence of this job segregation is that women are concentrated in the more labour-intensive and lower-paid jobs and industries. And often it was these very jobs which were the first to be mechanised.

According to Chapkis and Enloe, "Whatever the particular process used to produce... in a given period or culture, women are allowed by men to perform only those tasks that correspond to their presumed 'natural' inclinations. And those tasks 'just happen' to be the ones receiving the least training, the least money and the least opportunity for advancement or public recognition. These are also the jobs that leave women most vulnerable to sexual harassment and lay-offs at the work place and to powerlessness within the family. Thus, keeping women in their place in the production process also serves to keep them in their place in society at large."[10]

Trade unions seem to accept these equations as they have never challenged them systematically. This has been discussed explicitly or implicitly in many of the articles here.

(4)   The Report of the Committee on the Status of Women, 1974, stated *automation* as an important reason for the decrease in women workers in the organised sector.[11] In many industries, like textile, pharmaceuticals, etc. this was a dual process. Jobs where women were traditionally employed e.g. cotton cleaning, reeling, and winding in cotton textiles, packing and assembly in pharmaceuticals, electronics, etc., were drastically reduced due to automation of labour-intensive,

repetitive stages of the production process.

Employers find girls quick to achieve proficiency in certain tasks because they are *already* trained in the art of manual dexterity. But because this training hasn't cost employers anything, it tends to go unrecognised. It is attributed to nature and it is not reflected in any higher pay.[12]

Secondly, the vast majority of jobs where women were not traditionally employed, remained shut for women. Thus a reduction in the number of jobs open to women was inevitable. In fact, in some plants and industries, even in jobs which remained, women were replaced by men which resulted in an even greater reduction in the number of women employed.

An area of double discrimination which women face regarding employment pertains to "heavy work". According to ILO recommendations (Maximum Weight Recommendation, 1967, No. 128), states like Maharashtra and Madras have prescribed a maximum weight to be carried by women. Women are not allowed to be assigned to regular transport of loads. In principle, legislation also prohibits the employment of women on load transport during pregnancy and for 10 weeks following confinement.

However in the informal sector, as well as in their household duties, women have been traditionally assigned the heaviest of work eg., carrying of headloads of water for long distances, manual grinding of corn, carrying heavy headloads in construction, mining and quarrying, etc. Only when these heavy operations are mechanised, they are automatically taken over by men, eg., mechanically grinding corn is almost exclusively done by men.

The story seems familiar: women are said to be *unfit* for heavy manual work and discriminated against in certain jobs like engineering. Where machines replace heavy manual work with comparatively lighter supervisory functions, women are termed 'unskilled' and are discriminated against, all over again.

This second aspect could possibly be due to some notion of *prestige* attached to working with machines, probably because machines embody a much greater amount of capital.[13] This is another area where capitalist and patriarchal values coalesce to undermine, underevaluate and underrate women's labour and skills.

(5)   Another important reason for discrimination against women in the organised sector is the employers' assessment of *women workers in the organised sector as the most expensive and least flexible* type of

labour force. An important 'reason' for this is ironically, the struggles of women workers and unions. The struggles of woman workers described in this volume in industries like textiles, jute, pharmaceuticals, as well as those in the beedi, cashew, coir industry, etc., were for more human conditions of work and life, for their rights as well as against the long dawn-to-dusk working hours, abysmal wage levels, lack of any facilities, and the arbitrary hire-and-fire policies of employers. These have been challenged over the last century and the result is some regulation in conditions of work as well as pay levels.

Over the years, after long struggle women workers in the organised sector have been able to win certain crucial facilities and benefits - regulations of working hours, maternity benefits, creches, ban on shift work, etc. These have been crucial for women as their work at the factory or office constitutes only half of their total work which also includes housework and childcare. As this is not true of men, men are often more prepared to work overtime for long hours often working double shifts, Lack of responsibility at home renders men 'more flexible'. This is an important reason why women pose greater resistance to compulsory overtime or increasing workloads.

However, the situation is almost diagonally opposite in the unorganised sector. Here, legal rights of the workforce are much weaker and unions virtually absent. Women in the unorganised sector have no benefits at all and often have to work for long hours and even on night shifts. Here their domestic role is completely and deliberately ignored. However, in another sense, the domestic role is reinforced as women are supposed to be only secondary wage-earners merely supplementing the male wage and hence can afford to work for less wages. Studies have shown that on the contrary, women working in the unorganised sector are forced to continue working there despite the appalling conditions, because they have no other choice; many are often the sole-earners in the family and this very dependence on their wages makes them more vulnerable to accept miserably low wages and bad working conditions.

Thus emerges a picture where women in the organised sector are from the employers' point of view, the most expensive and the least flexible of the entire labour force, while women in the unorganised sector are the least expensive and the most flexible.[14]

Thus it may not be true to say that women's employment in industry as a whole is declining. Many of the big companies, including multinational companies which stopped recruiting women years ago are now sub-contracting out parts of their production process to smaller units where women are often employed in large numbers, and are sometimes in the majority. This loss of jobs in the organised industry is also true of men but the scale as well as the logic behind the two is different as outlined above. The new jobs in the unorganised industry however, are under employment conditions very different from those which were lost since they are in a sector where the Factories Act and other legislative provisions do not apply and which is largely un-unionised.

This transfer of jobs, especially women's jobs, from the organised to the unorganised sector is found to take place in almost every industry and very different strategies are used by employers to effect this transfer. These industries range from beedi-rolling and slate-pencil making to cloth production, pharmaceuticals and engineering.

Implications of unorganised workforce

The un-unionised nature of the workforce has a number of implications:
(i)   Workers in this sector work and live in appalling conditions and are barely able to live a human existence.
(ii)   The more widespread and scattered this sector, the more difficult it becomes to organise or to better one's conditions.
(iii) This sector is created to afford employers more bargaining power and control not only vis-a-vis the unorganised sector, but also the organised sector as the employers become less and less dependent on the organised workforce.
(iv)   This threatens to reverse the earlier process. Earlier workers in newly established plants were struggling to organise themselves and to assert their aspirations which gradually over decades became consolidated into fairly strong unions. Now, even big and hitherto strong unions have begun to buckle under pressure from employers and many unions have been forced to sign fairly dangerous and humiliating conditions, eg., a ceiling on Dearness Allowance, flexibility clauses, and implicit understanding of not recruiting women, while the general recruitment has also slackened considerably.

It has been argued that decentralisation implies more even development and balanced distribution of employment opportunities. However, the way this 'decentralisation' is taking place is that it is basically big industrial houses like the Tatas, Levers, Ambanis etc., who are setting up facilities in remote rural and backward areas to avail of the massive concessions offered by the Government and the financial institutions. Thus, even in this 'decentralisation', capital is still concentrated and centralised. It is only labour which is being decentralised. The new workers recruited in the rural areas have no experience of industry and unionisation. They have been refused any access to the unionised workers of the parent plants. The employers on the other hand, have the experience of dealing with workers. Thus, capital is highly centralised and labour decentralised and rendered weaker - exactly the opposite of what would imply the democratisation of industry.[15]

Struggles in industry

Despite heavy odds-workers and especilly women workers have struggled on various issues consistently. Some of the most persistent issues in industry have been security of employment, living wage, regulation of hours of work, basic facilities and allowances, discriminatory treatment ,etc. One of the earlier struggles that was waged was over the right of workers to organise themselves. Textile workers were one of the first sections in this country to take up some of these issues. As discussed in the earlier section, they were the first ones to struggle for reducing the inhuman, long working hours and also to struggle for the introduction of Dearness Allowance (DA) to compensate for the continuous erosion of their living standards by inflationary prices.The women textile workers also fought in the 1930s against discriminatory treatment regarding employment of women as discussed in this volume.

Women workers in the jute industry in West Bengal have also had a long history of struggle as discussed in Saswati Ghosh's article in this volume. Women workers have struggled on other issues too. In Nipani, beedi workers fought the employers who were trying to dismiss workers on the basis of age. One employer conducted medical examinations, declared women unfit and retrenched them without any compensation. As most women had no proof of their age, the management got the doctors to certify their ages and then declared them unfit for work. The Chikodi Taluka Kamgar Union, registered in 1980 and with a membership of around 2,000 women tobacco workers

demanded that no retrenchment would be allowed without workers
being paid compensation for the number of years of service and in the
absence of such provision, women would continue to work.[16]

Another important struggle was that of the Chattisgarh Mines
Sangharsh Samiti (CMSS) on the issue of Voluntary Retirement
specifically aimed at women.[17] The Voluntary Retirement Scheme,
mooted in 1976, proposed that a women worker below 57 years could
voluntarily retire at any age and nominate her male relative to take her
job and position. The scheme resulted in large scale buying of women's
job especially in tribal area by middle class non-tribal men having
fake marriages with tribal women. Most unions have been blissfully
unaware that this constitutes a blatant discrimination against women
workers. One union - the CMSS, with a membership of over 8,000
contract labourers and the women's wing of the union, the Mahila Mukti
Morcha, linked up the issue of voluntary retirement with the larger
issue of mechanisation and its effects on women. CMSS mobilised and
conscientised women and men and took up a systematic campaign to
formulate strategies against such schemes.

Struggles in other areas of employment

Struggles of women workers are not restricted to industry alone. The
struggles of women vendors as analysed by Renana Jhabvala and of
fishworkers by Aleyamma Vijayan in this volume are a few instances.
Struggles of women in rural employment have been discussed in another
volume. It would suffice here to indicate the range of issues taken up
by these sections of women.

Women have been active in various movements like the struggles
to demand land,[18] water, right to forests[19] and to work[20] to mention
only a few. Historically, from colonial times, there have been many
struggles waged by peasants and labourers like the Tebhaga movement
in West Bengal (1946-50),[21] the Telangana struggle in Andhra Pradesh
(1946-51),[22] tribal protests against forest encroachment during the 19th
and 20th centuries, etc. From documented material it is known that
women participated militantly in all these protests.

Women continue to struggle. Various organisations of rural labourers
and tribals all over the country have sprung up in the 1970s and the
1980s. The Kashtakari Sanghatana, Shramik Sanghatana,[23] the Shramjivi
Sanghatana and many others in Maharashtra have been known for very

strong women's participation. The Chipko movement [24] (1972) in Uttarkhand, the Appiko movement in Karnataka[25] (1983) have been dominated by women and women's concerns.

Legal struggles

Women workers and unions have very consciously adopted a multipronged approach in their struggle. On the one hand, they have mobilised themselves, attempted to organise in unions/organisations; they have raised demands, negotiated peacefully, signed agreements, also staged demonstrations, marches and organised campaigns. One element in this multi-pronged approach has been the legal area. This consciousness has increased and taken shape in the last few decades, though one observes that struggles have been fought even much earlier.

Legal struggle is by no means easy; in fact, it is often isolating, demoralising and taxing, both financially and emotionally. Yet women have refused to give in. One of the earliest legal battles on work-related areas was fought on the issue of the so-called 'marriage clause'. However, more recently, more and more sections of women are coming forward and challenging discriminatory treatment.

Legal struggles are especially important, because *case law* is an important determinant in the interpretation, reinterpretation and extension of legislative provisions. Case law is an important *source* of law pertaining to employment discrimination, the others being the constitution, legislation and common law.

Women workers have fought legal battles on the following issues, among others, and won important victories:

(1)   Striking down of the 'no-marriage' clause.

An important struggle of pharmaceutical women workers and their unions has been described in an article in this volume. There have been many others during the same period - the early 1960s.

In another case, Bombay Labour Union vs. International Franchise (AIR 1966 SC 9421), the Court pointed out that the ban on women's recruitment had no nexus to job performance since concerns about absenteeism and maternity leave were insignificant.

(2)   Striking down the validity of the regulations specifying that women would be terminated if they became pregnant.

The Supreme Court struck down the regulation in the case of Air India vs. Nargeesh Meerza (AIR 1981 SC 1829), under article 14 as "a most unreasonable and arbitrary provision which shocks the conscience of the court."

(3) Striking down of policies like designating jobs as male without providing any justification, or laying down unnecessary conditions which women would not be able to fulfill.

In case of A.H.Ranjamma vs. State of Kerala (1983 Lab.I.C.,1988,1896), the Kerala High Court struck down the policy of designating most of the jobs as male without providing any justification. The court stated that it should be the woman's individual decision whether she wants to apply for a given job:' if the work... does not suit a woman or she would feel humiliated by such work. It is for her to decide whether to apply for the concerned job and not for the male dominated legislature or the male dominated hierarchy.'

Some of the other issues[26] on which women workers/employees have waged legal struggles are:

(4) Challenging discrimination against women because of hours of work and association with male officers in the case of Vijayamma vs. State of Kerala (977 Ker.L.T. 677)

(5) Challenging the requirement for the consent of the husband before employing women as in the case of Maya Devi vs. State of Maharashtra (1986 Lab.I.C.793).

(6) Challenging discrimination in pay though the work is of a similar nature, as in the case of MacKinnon and Mackenzie vs. Audrey D'Costa (AIR 1987 SC 1281).

(7) Another issue that women have bravely taken up is that of sexual harrassment, e.g., in the case of A.Santhakumar vs. Regional Dir., Postal Services, Kurnool (1982, Lab.I.C. 1756(AP)).

Women have legally and otherwise taken up many more issues, often isolatedly, sometimes collectively. The perseverance of women workers/employees is all the more surprising, as even a victory in the struggle or in the courts is not always an unmixed one; even a partial victory is often difficult and the struggle daunting. Eg., in the case of C.B.Muthamma vs. Union of India, discussed above, while the court ruled in favour of the woman, in the same judgment, the Supreme Court .suggested certain factors that might permit employers to treat women employees unfavourably:

"We do not mean to universalise and dogmatise that men and women are equal in all situations and do not exclude the need to pragmatize where in the requirement of a particular employment, the sensitivities of sex or the peculiarities of societal sectors or the handicaps of either sex may compel selectivity."

The same situation exists with respect to most of our 'victories'. These fairly sharp ups and downs are all the more true of non-legal struggles—at the shop-floor level, on the streets, in the fields and in the market. It is these struggles, individual and collective, that determine the lives and the morale of struggling people, also women.

Most factors that determine the success and defeat of these struggles are not within the control of women. Often, women seem to be struggling for an issue, a cause which is moral, human and legal. Yet the outcome of the struggle is very rarely a positive one for women. However, the *process of struggle* seems to be as important, if not more important, than the outcome. That is one reason why despite severe hardships and obstacles, women continue to struggle on different issues and on the same issues anew.

Factors determining struggles of women

Many factors contribute to the ability and willingness of women to struggle. The important bases of most struggles are - (1) a sense of being wronged; (2) assertion of their own dignity and self respect; (3) a sense of self preservation and a need to better their situation in the given circumstances and possibly, to change these circumstances themselves.

An important factor in women's decision to participate in a particular struggle at a specific point in time is the *expected outcome* of the struggle, though this may not be the only factor. The expected outcome itself depends on several factors. While some of these factors are common to men and women workers, others affect specifically women. Some of these are:

(a) Women's judgment of their own individual/collective strength vis-a-vis that of their employer.

This judgment may depend upon the employer's need for that particular workforce in terms of skill and experience needed in the work process.

In situations like the garment industry discussed by Rukmini Rao and Sahba Husain in this volume, where employers resort to closing down one plant and opening others without much difficulty at the slightest sign of unionisation, the workers are often a little slow to organise. This situation is prevalent in many industries, eg., beedi-making, cashew nut, coir processing, where employers are closing down factories and giving out production to women at home. Organising is many times more difficult in these situations.

Also, recently' in the case of the pharmaceutical plants, textile and jute units discussed in this volume, where employers have opened up parallel units or want to close down for other reasons, struggles have at least a more defensive tone than in earlier periods.

(b)   Another important aspect is women's economic dependence on the employer.

Unmarried women with no dependents and married women with husbands who earn a decent salary or those who have grown-up independent children are in the strongest position, and are often prepared to participate in struggles without much fear of the consequences. The risk of losing their only means of livelihood, of seeing their children suffer and of getting enslaved forever to money-lenders is a strong disincentive to participation in struggles. This is all the more acute because of the insecure nature of women's employment, which means that to enter a struggle almost certainly means getting thrown out and finding it more difficult to get another job, which would be no better than the present one and in all likelihood, much worse.

This situation is all the more serious in the unorganised sector as discussed in this volume for the garment industry by Rukmini Rao and Sahba Husain, the women contract workers of a thermal power station by Priya and for beedi workers Renana Jhabvala. The beedi workers of Patan were at first reluctant to take any confrontational steps as there were no other alternative employment possibilities in Patan and beedi work was an important source of income for their families. This fear also exists in the organised sector in different forms as the 1982 textile strike has adequately proved, or the threats that Tamil Nadu teachers had to withstand during their strike, as discussed by Vasanti Devi in her article in this volume.

In countries like India, where more than one-third of women are sole or main supporters of their families, women's economic dependence on their employers is very high. Often, where women almost entirely support their families, the control of the family on them is greater, not less. It does not give women freedom to choose whether and how they want to participate; very often it is decided for them by the menfolk who are dependent on women for their survival.

However, according to Shaswati Mazumdar's account in this volume of the 1982 and 1985-86 strike of the Delhi University Teachers' Association (DUTA), where women teachers were secondary income-earners, they responded less to mobilisation on purely economic issues. Such teachers were far more active on issues of democratic rights, education policy, etc.

(c)   The third factor determining women's ability and willingness to struggle is **their being able to identify a common institution, or person or set of persons, who are responsible for the present situation or a change in it.**

Workplaces like factories provide a material basis for a process of struggle. The most fundamental way in which it does this is by bringing together large numbers of women and confronting them with a common, cash-based authority: the authority of capital. Here, both struggle and solidarity are with a determinate set of people.

Most employment situations of women in countries like ours — unremunerated labour in the family, work in the 'informal sector', in homebased industries, etc. — do not however, offer these material bases. Women tend to be physically isolated from one another, or do not have an idea of who they can raise their demands with, or they are confronted with different, more personalised forms of authority - 'auntiji', 'uncleji', 'didi', in the garment industry; jobbers in the textile industry; their own male colleagues in the fishworkers' struggle discussed by Aleyamma Vijayan and in the air-hostesses' struggle by Rohini Gawaskar in this volume. Often, women do not even have an image of themselves as workers and of other workers as their colleagues or work-mates, as is the case with a large number of home-based workers. So also the garment workers.

However, the situation seems to be changing as is shown by SEWA's attempts at organising both vendors and beedi-workers in Ahmedabad. In these attempts, a new concept of unions seems to be emerging. It implies a more complex concept of struggle against an authority and a process of solidarity among different sections of workers.

(d) The fourth element in determining women's struggles, **is women's experience of participation in earlier struggles.**

Many women go into their first struggle with enthusiasm, but bitterly regret it if it ends in defeat. Some of the reactions of the beedi workers at Patan are of this nature. Also of some of the garment workers.

Some come out of it feeling that struggle only makes a bad situation worse, and that it is better to remain quiet. Both the experiences of beedi workers at Patan and of some of the garment workers are of this type. Many small-scale industry workers, contract workers, rural labourers too have experienced this in the initial phase of their organising.

Some others feel that outside leaders are not to be trusted, they make use of workers and then leave them in the lurch; and as for male worker-leaders, they are better, but ultimately women workers have to rely on their own strength. This was the experience of the garment workers regarding outside unions. In the women teachers' struggle in Tamil Nadu however, women felt that their trust in the commitment and sincerity of the leadership was an important factor which sustained their morale and willingness to continue the struggle.

Sometimes women feel utterly helpless, because although they are prepared to continue the fight and feel that they have to struggle in order to improve their own conditions, they have no idea how to do so. While the beedi workers of Patan had no earlier experience of organisation or struggle, the beedi workers in Ahmedabad who were largely immigrants from Andhra Pradesh, where their mothers and grandmothers had been active in unions, were prepared to unionise and had already been thinking about it.

Another reaction is one of exhilarated enthusiasm. Women are prepared, as in the case of the Tamil Nadu women teachers, to participate in another struggled with renewed enthusiasm, despite their having experienced imprisonment and state repression. The old-clothes' sellers described in Renana Jhabwala's article were jubilant when they won against the police and proceeded to form an organisation, which in turn awakened in the vegetable vendors a need to organise themselves under SEWA and they took on the police, municipal authorities and fought upto the Supreme Court.

Lastly, women workers, after participation in a struggle, often sit back, rethink individually and collectively of their own mistakes, their weaker areas and strong points and after a period of time get back into struggle, or at least are prepared to do so.

(e) **Experiences of other earlier struggles of women or workers in the industry or area** are an important determinant too. This could also loosely be termed the **'culture of struggle'** in the industry/area.

This is a process of collectively evaluating their strength vis-a-vis that of the employers and sharpening their tools of struggle. This is a long drawn-out historical process and often has a cyclical pattern. The struggles of women workers in the textile, jute, and mining area have been documented over the years. This volume too looks at two of these struggles.

Historical perspective or tradition has been an important aspect in women's struggle. What, however, determines the nature of contemporary struggle is also the general atmosphere of the workplace.

If there are many women and a general air of militancy, women participate actively in struggle, where as if women are few and isolated, they become more passive. This is the experience of women in the organised pharmaceutical industry, where while they had struggled enthusiastically in the earlier period when they were in a majority, now they are less willing to do so.

In the case of the Chhattisgarh mine workers' union, "Once a large number of women were mobilised, they acted as a pressure group for the formulation of struggle issues from a women's perspective. For instance in the Chhattisgarh mines, the particular way in which the mechanisation issue was formulated as something that for ideological reasons, selectively affects women, was because of a union membership that was half female."[27]

Again a huge upheaval like a state-wide strike, eg., the teachers' strike or an industry-wide strike, eg., the textile strike, which is either partially successful or severely repressed can activate many women who had not earlier participated in a strike before.

(f) Often, **the general atmosphere prevalent in the community** is an important factor in the willingness of women to participate in collective struggles. At times even when the issue is important and crucial, it draws no response; at other times women are up in arms and that wipes out or at least minimises the weight of obstacles in their way.

This was certainly the situation in the case of the Tamil Nadu teachers' struggle when married women, women with very small children left them behind in the care of husbands, in-laws and friends to participate in the struggle. For many of them, this was their first experience in collective action and yet even a couple of years after the struggle they remember their days in prison as an experience that was "intense, beautiful and elevating".

(g) However, often the **nature and content of work** is such that women workers do not feel justified in resorting to certain types of struggles, eg., work-stoppages. This has often been observed with nurses, teachers and people who directly deal with or serve others, especially people who are needy or not responsible for the plight of the women.

This was the case with certain sections of women teachers in the Delhi DUTA strike of 1985 as discussed in this volume.

This is also because this is how society and the State pressurise women workers - trying to 'appeal to their conscience' about the implications of their actions on innocent people, not responsible for the bad situation the women are in. Shaswati Mazumdar also comments on the deliberate narrow sense in which this commitment has been defined by vested interests.

(h) The **attitude of the State - the police, administration, courts -** also determines women workers' participation in struggles. There is of course no linear process of determination. During the 1982 textile strike as well as the 1974 railway strike, women workers were very well aware of possible repression by the State. Yet they participated enthusiastically in large numbers with grim determination. However, as time went on and there was no sign of the State budging an inch, women and men workers began to feel a little hesitant. In the 1974 railway strike, the extent and **type** of repression was brutal and severe, including eviction of workers' families from housing colonies and rapes of women. Rapes are often used especially in more remote areas against striking women workers or militant women. This is intended to strike at the morale of the women and men.

In certain instances like the women teachers' struggle, the State unleashed repression, but the nature of it - imprisoning women teachers en masse - possibly helped solidarity. Thousands of women teachers came out to picket and court arrest. A majority of them "rose against what they perceived to be gross injustice done to them in terms of pay scales and service conditions". The same is true of the Delhi teachers' struggle in which they were threatened with both a wage cut and a change in their service conditions.

Repression unleashed on very poor, non-permanent employees has graver consequences, as their source of livelihood is threatened and that too in a situation when people's existence is almost a hand-to-mouth one. Yet the contract workers of the thermal power plant in Tamil Nadu discussed by Priya in this volume fought out even in the courts with some success.

Similarly, existence of legal provisions on an issue contributes positively to women's participation in and attitude to struggle. For example, women workers' struggle in most parts of Maharashtra for the implementation of the Minimum Wages Act took a much greater momentum. This is because in one's consciousness 'legal' also means what is sanctioned by the State and society and therefore what is one's right.

(i) The **political situation in the area, industry, country and often at the international level** is an important factor contributing to workers' morale to struggle.

In the history of the workers' movement nationally as well as internationally, one sees distinct phases of struggle in different periods.

One of the earliest periods discussed in this volume is the period of the late 1920s, just before the Great Depression of the 1930s. Struggles raged in the textile and the jute industry.

A majority of articles in this volume discuss struggles of women in the period after the wave of the post-1960s, when at an international level, various sections of society were organising themselves into movements and making their voices heard - the black movement, the women's movement, the anti-war movement, various industrial and students' actions which culminated in the May 1968 movements.

The drought of the early 1970s also spurred these movements in the Western part of the country. Another important period is the post-Emergency period which saw a major upheaval.

The teachers' Association in Delhi too acquired a new life after the defeat of the party that had imposed the Emergency. The Association became more active after 1979-80 and engaged in mass scale actions for the realisation of their Charter of Demands.

(j) An important element is also **women workers' self-evaluation of their own labour.**

This may also refer to the recognition or otherwise of the skills and indispensability that women workers may feel they possess vis-a-vis the employers. However, women workers have a distinct disadvantage in this respect, not because they do not possess skills by nature or are easily dispensable as a rule, but because of the low social valuation of their skills and role in the production process.

Skill categories are not determined in a purely objective way. In particular, jobs which are identified as women's work tend to be classified as 'unskilled' or 'semi-skilled', whereas technically similar jobs identified as 'men's work' tend to be classified as 'skilled'. "To a large extent, women do not do 'unskilled' jobs because they are the bearers of inferior labour, rather the jobs they do are 'unskilled' because women enter them already determined as inferior bearers of labour."[28]

In industries like garments, women workers are termed unskilled. Even work like embroidering is so evaluated. This is also because employers have not spent any time or capital in training the women; women have learnt it from their mothers or grand-mothers possibly for several years. This training or transferance of skills does not need to be recognised because both the 'trainers' and the 'trainees' are women.

(k) The **attitude and reactions of the family** are important considerations for women in deciding whether they would participate in struggles and to what extent, i.e., whether they would be leading decision-makers and activists or participants. Support from families sustained the Tamil Nadu teachers' 42-day strike and the Delhi teachers' 109-day strike in 1982 and the 74-day strike in 1985-86. Pressure from home is extremely crucial. In the case of garment workers, Godavari had to withdraw because of her husband's disapproval of her participation. This is a theme that recurs in all accounts of women workers' struggles, while in the accounts of predominantly male workers' struggles, it is invariably the case that their wives and families are extremely involved and they too participate whether it is the coal-miners' strike in the UK, or the nationwide railway strike in 1974 or the TELCO strike in Pune in 1989. The struggle then takes on the form of not only an industrial dispute, but that of a political struggle with community involvement.

This is the converse of the stereotyped picture we have - i.e., that of the wife who holds back her husband from struggle - and suggests very strongly that this stereotype is thoroughly misleading. If there are more documented cases of wife holding back her husband from struggle than the opposite, this is surely because in our society, it is generally the man of the family who is employed in the organised sector and it is generally struggles in this sector which are widely reported and discussed.

(l) Often women workers have no illusions about the outcome of the struggle, nor is the objective situation in favour of the women at that moment. However, **women are desperate;** they have taken it lying low for too long: "enough is enough" is what they feel and plunge in.

The 1982 textile strike was one such struggle. It has been argued by many labour researchers that the timing of the strike was not opportune. Workers usually are aware of such factors. But they had tolerated too long the injustice of the Bombay Industrial Relations Act (BIR Act) in not allowing them to choose their own representatives. They wanted to fight whatever the outcome. In many small scale factories, where no legislation is applicable, women are known to have braved all sorts of threats and obstacles. In the Santacruz Electronics Export Processing Zone (SEEPZ), Bombay, where young women constitute over 90 per cent of the workforce, women have struggled for long periods in order to form a union; many have lost their jobs; some, after 5 years, are still fighting legal battles. Even the women of the newer units are trying to organise themselves.[29]

Women are known to have struggled for long periods of time even in the unorganised sector in remote areas where might is right and even a struggle for minimum wages has turned violent and been severely repressed.

(m) A slight variation of this situation of desperation is **the feeling that if you don't struggle now, anyway you are bound to lose; you might as well plunge in.**

Similar feelings have been expressed by women workers in the pharmaceutical industry and other places when women fought against the 'marriage clause'. Or by the garment workers when they realised that their loyalty had not paid off and they were retrenched and would lose even their back wages if they did not do anything just then.

The women workers in a jeans factory in Greenock, Scotland, occupied their workplace in an attempt to stop their company from closing down. The determination with which the women resisted the closure was strengthened by the knowledge that there was little chance of finding another job and many women's families were dependent on their wages.[30]

(n) **Through their own experience, women realise that many of the issues they face cannot be addressed by them individually.** They have struggled individually and that is just not enough.

This is obvious to women in situations like that of the beedi workers, old-clothes' sellers, vegetable vendors, contract workers, garment workers, etc., when they have to confront a much more powerful, hostile and organised force or institution. However, women also realise the need to come together as women and struggle for some autonomy in mixed organisations, eg., women fishworkers in Kerala who formed the Coastal Women's Front with a great deal of struggle - against themselves, their menfolk and their own organisation.

Often women feel the need to express themselves, their suppressed talents, the need to know more than their immediate environment would allow. Once a part of struggle and organisation, they begin to see newer aspects of their own personality, a flowering of their own self-confidence, as happened with the women fishworkers.

(o) There have been many instances where the reasons put forward by women workers in struggle seem to be different and often out of proportion as compared to the actual actions they initiate or participate in. In these cases, the struggle may not have an immediate cause or the immediate reason given may be a rationalisation. The actual 'reasons' may be different. This may be termed **struggle as protest against an entire sum total of situations women have had to face earlier.**

These often take the form of flash strikes or flash sit-ins. These have been elaborately documented in the case of the electronics industries in many third world countries. These have also taken the form of fainting or 'mass hysteria' which may begin with one or two women and may spread throughout the production floor. These have also been discussed briefly in this volume when the textile workers went on strike in 1926 because they did not want to use cheese winding machines. Radha Kumar describes this as 'women workers were resisting the alienation capitalism brought in tow".

Another such strike described in the same article took place when the European manager touched the food basket of one of the women and 'polluted' it. This could be one not-so-unacceptable way of getting back at managers who otherwise treated women badly!

(p) Women workers' ability and willingness to struggle also depends on **whether and how they can translate their interests into structured associations.**

This however is not easy, because for women workers to gain a sense of cohesion is much more difficult than for all workers to do so. "Workers are bound together by a community of interests which are distinctly and obviously different from those of employers; in their normal day-to-day life, familiar social contact is with other workers not employers."[31]

Similarly, other sections of people, eg., dalits, too share a community of interests - their historical experience, their present status. Their oppression is something society frowns upon as not moral, not legal. However, for women, even employed women, their identity as women workers is only one of their many identities, but one aspect of their lives and roles. In their other roles, which perhaps are as important if not more, they are divided and separated from each other. In most of the occupations women work in, they are physically isolated from one another. They tend not to relate to one another as members of the same gender or class, but as members of particular households and kin groups.[32]

Besides, as Jockes and Baud put it, "Time is gendered - inside the factory and inside the family - and it takes time to organise... The family-factory relationship implies a different strategy of action for women workers."[33] This however is not impossible as women workers' organisations in Nepal, Pakistan, the Phillipines and Korea have shown.

In India too, the experience of Coastal Women's Front in the South and the Mahila Mukti Morcha in the North among others have succeeded in consolidating women's struggles and aspirations into organisational forms. These have made a systematic and consistent programme for the women possible.

(q) **The strength women derive from the process of struggle is** also an important determinant. Women are able to express themselves openly and probably demonstrate even to themselves their capabilities and capacities which were hitherto invisible.

In the Chhattisgarh movement for example, the entire process of meetings, regular democratic elections and freedom of speech that women experienced in the organisation represented a tremendous political and personal achievement for them. Many other movements would provide similar examples.[34] As Norma 'Corky' Jennings , a woman unionist in the U.S., put it, "Union work always helped keep me sane."[35]

To sum up, the ability and willingness of women to struggle is determined by a number of factors. The important bases of most struggles are:

1.   a sense of self-preservation and a need to better their own situation;

2.   assertion of their own dignity and self-respect;
3.   a sense of being wronged and an urge to right the wrong.

An important factor in women's decision to participate in a particular struggle is the *expected outcome* of the struggle, though this may not be the only factor. The expected outcome itself may depend upon several factors:

(a)   women's judgment of their own collective strength vis-a-vis that of their employer;

(b)   women's economic dependence on the employer;

(c)   women's ability to identify a common institution/person/set of persons responsible for their situation or a change in it;

(d)   women's experience of participation in earlier struggles;

(e)   experience of other earlier struggles of women or workers in the industry or area, that is, culture/tradition of struggle;

(f)   the general atmosphere prevalent in the community;

(g)   nature and content of women's work;

(h)   response of the State, legislature, police, etc.,

(i)   the political situation in the area, industry, country, and often at the international level;

(j)   self-evaluation of women's own role in production;

(k)   attitude and reactions of the family, neighbours, etc.;

(l)   desperate situation of women, they have taken it lying low for too long;

(m)   the feeling that if you don't struggle now, anyway you are bound to lose; you might as well plunge in;

(n)   through their own experience, women realise that many of the issues they face cannot be addressed by them individually;

(o)   struggle as protest against an entire sum total of situations women have had to face earlier;

(p)   whether and how women workers can translate their interests into structured association;

(q)   the strength women derive from the process of struggle.

Women workers and organisations

In the unorganised sector, where 94 per cent women workers are employed, the completely unprotected status of women workers, legally and in actual reality has rendered self-organisation difficult. Women workers have attempted again and again to organise, to protest, to struggle. Their attempts have often been frustrated, sometimes brutally crushed. Their only means of survival has been snatched from them. Repeated failures and defeats sometimes give rise to passivity and fatalism however momentary, as has been discussed in the article in this volume on garment workers.

Diane Elson and Ruth Pearson have discussed some of these issues: "Fanon shows how the public passivity and fatalism which the colonised people displayed towards the colonisers for long periods contained an inner, private rebellion and subversion. But this passivity is not a natural and original state: to achieve it requires enormous efforts of self-repression. The 'native' is in a state of permanent tension, so that when he does resist it tends to be with a spontaneity and intensity all the stronger for having been so long pent up and hidden. Action, not negotiation, is the characteristic response." (*Fanon,* 1968, p. 48)

"That self-repression is required for women to achieve an adequate level of docility and subservience can be demonstrated on an every day level by differences in their behaviour when authority figures are present and absent. An example is the behaviour observed by Heyzer (1978) in a world market factory producing textiles in Singapore."[36]

Self-repression or repression by employers and the State, a sense of survival, of dignity, a strong feeling of being wronged and desperation urge women workers to express their anger, their protest. Often hoping to 'win', but conscious also of the powers against them, they resort to direct action. "Though their level of participation in trade unions is reported to be very low, there are indications that the struggles tend to erupt outside the official trade union framework, taking for instance, the form of 'wild-cat' strikes or sit-downs or walk-outs, rather than being organised around official negotiations."[37]

In most literature on unions or by unions, especially more recently, there are references to the non-participation of women in trade unions, women's 'apathy' to trade unions, etc., as discussed in the article on trade unions in this volume.

However, many of the other articles in this volume suggest that women workers have gained enormous victories through organisation in unions. The women workers in the pharmaceutical industry in Bombay, through their unions have won important demands like a shorter working week, creche facilities, maternity benefits; they have been able to put an end to blatantly discriminatory service conditions like early retirement and retrenchment soon after marriage. The same is true of air-hostesses. The textile workers were the first sections to struggle for the historical Dearness Allowance. The beedi workers could get the legislative machinery to pay attention to their demands, only because they were organised. Even those sections which are, objectively speaking, in an extremely weak position like the vendors did reach the gates of the Supreme Court.

How do these two situations -- one, of women's struggles through unions and two, of the very small percentage of women enrolled in unions, not to say the miniscule number in leadership positions --coexist? What may we derive out of this regarding the relationship of unions and women workers?

It is indeed difficult to deny the fact that trade unions have been and still are extremely important in the struggle of women to control their own lives. Through trade unions they have been able to increase the amount of time which is free from wage-work and gain considerable control over this part of their lives -- through higher income, better amenities and welfare provisions, etc. They have in some cases also managed to gain a certain degree of control over their wage-work itself.

However, despite the obvious importance and indispensability of trade unions for women wage workers in determining their own wages and working conditions, and for other women, in determining their family wage, it is commonly observed that women are less active and enthusiastic trade unionists than men. Few women are trade union members, fewer women who are members participate regularly in trade union activities, and even fewer are in positions of leadership in unions, as the paper on AITUC, CITU and INTUC by Nivedita Menon in this volume demonstrates.

Trade Unions and Women

There seem to be many, both historical and contemporary, reasons for this state of affairs. Well before the industrial revolution in the West or the development of capitalism in India, women, even when they laboured outside the home along with men, were held responsible for almost all the work involved in caring for children and running the home. This responsibility continued to increase with the decline or abolition of child labour, shorter working hours and higher living standards. This had to have a definite impact on their involvement and participation in wage-work struggles, since their attitude to wage-work would determine their attitude to the organisation based on that work, namely trade unions. This conception of childcare and housework as taking priority over both wage-work and trade unionism is based on the realisation that both at work and more so in the trade union they are dispensable -- someone else could do the job instead of them -- whereas at home, if, for example, the children have to be fed or are ill, there is no one else to look after them, and they are therefore indispensable.

From the earliest beginnings till today, both paid work (including wage-work, but also family-based occupations) and trade unions have been dominated by male workers. In fact, even before industrialisation, women have consistently been allotted a subordinate role within the traditional family-based handicrafts. Women were not allowed to belong to the ancient craft guilds although they assisted their husbands in their home workshops. This is also true of occupations like pottery, weaving, smithy, etc.

Later, after the advent of industrialisation, men workers worked against the interests of women -- by excluding them from membership, by campaigning against their entry into wage-work, by isolating them. In countries where trade unions were formed before being formed in India, like in England, Germany etc., the early history of trade unions is a struggle not only against employers for trade union demands and recognition, but also against women. Women workers there had to form separate trade unions of women. These were fairly successful in organising women and in winning important demands for women workers. It was only under their pressure that trade unions began to open their doors to women.[38]

The issue here is a dual one: I) the limited perception of trade unions regarding their own role -- historical and contemporary: II) the phenomenon of male domination in trade unions still persists and the special issues of women are underplayed and hence their participation remains peripheral.

I) **The limited perception of unions** is reflected in various ways and has ultimately undermined its own strength.

(a) The attitude of unions regarding issues other than immediate wages and benefits has been one of indifference. Many unions have consciously avoided dealing with issues like promotions or recruitment in any other way than a purely reactive one, because of fear of competition and disunity within the workers. By and large, these issues have been looked at as 'management areas'. The perspective of the employers/ managements that apart from wages-benefits-retrenchment (unfair dismissal etc.), all other areas are management prerogatives has to varying extents been uncritically accepted by unions.

(b) While there has been a history of a joint management forum and offensive, the union movement has been fragmented and dispersed, without a coherent statement about the task of the changing times.

(c) Almost from the beginning of the trade union movement in this country (as in most other countries), men have been in the leadership of the unions and this single fact has had an impact on the issues taken up (or not taken up) and the manner in which they were taken up by the unions. Until more recently, men workers have not been seriously affected by the job-losses strategy of employers. In fact, in many instances when women lost jobs (either directly through retrenchment or indirectly through non-recruitment), it was men who benefitted as more men were recruited in place of women. Only recently have a) machines been replacing men and to some extent women, and b) women and men in the unorganised sector have been replacing both men and women in the organised sector.

This trend is merely an extension of the earlier one which victimised largely women. The employers seem to have felt confident and strengthened in their successful attempt at reducing the number of women workers and more openly repeating it with the entire organised labour force.

(d) It is possible that this inability to challenge management practices also relates to the uncritical acceptance of a particular definition of 'a normal worker' given by employers. Eg., most union's arguments are restricted to 'permanent workers', while often temporary, casual, and contract workers are regarded as 'outsiders' and not allowed to become members of unions of permanent workers. A few unions include temporary workers as members, but the terms on which they work are far worse than those of the permanent workforce. Some unions have agreed to give services like canteen, company transport, sweeping and toilet-cleaning on contract. This **uncritical acceptance of the management definition of worker as permanent and male** could be one aspect of the problem. It has been pointed out that unions and books on unions make no reference to women workers at all. A leading labour academician's book is still more explicit - it is called 'The Worker and *His* Union'!

Hence the experience of contract workers vis-a-vis not only the management, but also the permanent workforce has not been quite positive. Women workers too have had similar experiences. Union leaderships do not seem to be sensitive to the various social pressures on women, like the sole responsibility women bear for all the housework, etc. and the lack of mobility imposed on them. The result of this has been that gradually women workers have taken less and less interest in union matters and as a result the problems they face are not taken up in unions as priority issues.

(e) Unions are primarily considered to be organisations responding to a specific relationship i.e., of wage labour and capital. However, as the articles in this volume elaborate, women work in situations which are much more complex.

Contract labourers ordinarily do not have one single identifiable employer; women vendors are self-employed; home-based workers may not know their employers. However, all of them have problems and interests which are common and several institutions which they have to struggle against. Hence there is the basis for an organisation like unions.

II) What is often debated is the infamous apathy of women to unions. The real issue however is apathy of unions to women. This could also include the problems within the basis and structure of unions.

The vast majority of working class women are excluded from unions. In theory, only those engaged in wage-work could belong to unions.

a) In practice this would be difficult given the marginal and insecure employment most women have to make do with.

b) Even if the massive task of unionising all female wage-workers were to be achieved, a very large section of working class women would still remain unorganised because their workplace is the home and they receive no wages.

c) Even for women wage-workers, their waged work is merely one part of their total working day and trade unions do not aim at dealing with issues relating to the other half of their work-life.

In the fishworkers' struggle described in this volume, earlier if the man had membership, it was presumed that his wife would participate in the union activities but she had no place in the official body. This was subsequently changed with pressure from women in Trivandrum.

Women were as active as the men, or more so, in the struggles of the fishworkers. But very few women actually came into positions of leadership. The structure of the union had a great deal to do with this. In the three-tier system it seemed obvious that only the men climbed to the top. Then, with meetings at some distance from home, the women often could not participate as they would not be given permission by their husbands to do so, or they themselves would have had problems about leaving their homes or their children. Meetings would also be late in the evening, often stretching into the night.

Even with respect to women wage-workers, trade unions do not deal with many of the problems they are seriously confronted with. Unions have often talked about women's inability to participate in unions and their household responsibilities. However, by and large, there have been no serious attempts to involve family members in such a way that women workers would get more support from them for union work. In fact, men workers/unionists have complained of the unwillingness of women to stay after work and participate in union activities. They completely fail to realise that the very reason that men *can* participate in union work -- their complete lack of responsibility at home -- renders women *unable* to do so.

There have not been attempts either to change union functioning to suit women's needs like scheduling union meetings at times convenient to women or making childcare facilities available at union functions, deliberately discussing women-related issues as priority areas, etc. This experience is common to sections and communities as varied as the fishworkers and pharmaceutical workers.

Issues like sexual harassment by colleagues, sexual division within the work place are not taken up by unions because of sexism within the organisations and a lack of perspective as indicated in the example of a pharmaceutical company in this volume. Also the lack of a conducive atmosphere during union activities is responsible, eg., physical violence, verbal indecency as in the Delhi teachers' union activities, leave alone the jeering women teachers had to experience when they suggested that the demand for creche facilities be included in the charter.

Issues like rape, sexual harassment on the streets, subordination within the family and restrictions on the freedom of movement, etc., are not taken up because they fall outside the area of issues the unions have defined for themselves. However, these issues affect women seriously, often completely curtailing their mobility. Women garment workers talked about the suspicion with which their neighbourhood looked at them when they came home late from union work or meetings.

In this situation, the implicit role of women workers as unions see it, is that of passive support for a male leadership. This is a role that most women have to play at home and in other areas of their life and unionism does not offer them any different role or function. When women do take initiative and act independently, the repercussions may be severe, generally taking the form of slander and persecution which may succeed in driving them out or shutting them up. Male leaders often look upon such women as threats rather than comrades-in-arms, as has been discussed in the experience of the pharmaceutical women leadership.

One way out of this, as the experience of women vendors and beedi workers in this volume suggests, is *exclusively women's unions.* Though the article in this volume does not go into this issue explicitly, it is well-known that women workers in SEWA have consciously voted for an exclusively women's union and organisation. Some of the reasons mentioned have been:

1.   Men tend to take over any activity or meeting even if they are not present in large numbers.

2.   Women's families as well as women will not feel as secure and safe if there are men around.

3.   Actions, meetings, etc., are decided according to the convenience of women; this will not remain so if the union is a mixed one.

As discussed earlier, women's unions were formed in the West when unions excluded women. However, once the unions were opened to women, exclusively women's trade unions gradually disappeared, despite the fact that women fared much worse in the mixed unions than they had in their own. In India, women's trade unions do not seem to have been prevalent at any time, possibly because trade unions in India were strongly influenced by the labour movement in Britain and were formed at a time when the major British unions were already open to women.

However, unions in the informal sector or newly organising workforces may be able to rethink about this strategy, given experiences like those of SEWA or the Working Women's Forum in Madras, or the less well known and newer organisations like the Ragpickers' Organisation in Baroda and possibly many more.

Another form of organisation that has been attempted is *women's cells or caucuses inside mixed trade unions.* The Mahila Mukti Morcha, the women's cell inside the Chattisgarh Mines Sangharsh Samiti (CMSS) is one of the many such attempts. In this volume, Aleyamma Vijayan discusses the experience of the Coastal Women's Front, a women's organisation linked with the Fishworkers' Union in Kerala. The Coastal Women's Front has taken up many issues related to women as workers (special transport facilities for women fish vendors), as women (rapes, murders), and as women workers (autonomy to decide their own issues, timing of union meetings, etc.)

In the fishworkers' organisation, the question of women not being allowed to rise to leadership positions was faced squarely and suggestions were made, eg., that rotational participation should be tried in the committees at the district level. The Tamil Nadu Construction Workers' Union has a women's wing. This was "formed in order to encourage women to participate in union activity."[39]

It is likely that many such organisational attempts and experiments are being tried out. The bases of these attempts at forming women's cells or caucuses inside mixed unions seem to be the following:

Firstly, to push for the *taking up of women's workplace issues* - eg., equal pay, abolition of sex-biased grading and exclusion of women from better jobs, training facilities for women, against sexual harassment, for creches, maternity and paternity benefits, specific work related issues like special transport facilities resistance to discrimination, etc.

Secondly, to *pressurise unions to support women's issues* raised outside the union, eg., housing for single women, and to take up the issue of atrocities on women, etc.

Thirdly, *to press for full participation of women* in the decision-making processes of the union, and to work for a change in the structure and functioning of the union to make this possible.

However, experiences like those of the contract workers and garment workers in this volume as well as those of home-based workers, suggests that although there is enough basis for these sections to organise as they suffer the worst employment conditions, they are prevented from organising to fight back by the fear of victimisation. As Renana Jhabvala puts it, "The harshest treatment is reserved for the poorest and neediest women, who are the most defenceless. So those who would really benefit from organising are the most fearful of doing so." This seems to point to the need for a *general women's union,* to help these women to draft their demands and section of if necessary, to struggle on their behalf through mass campaigns, etc. In one sense, SEWA is some version of such a union, as the basic infrastructure as well as concrete experience is there for women to come and avail of when they feel the need.

However, one also needs to take into account experiences like the nurses' union in Maharashtra and of other sections, where despite the fact that the leadership consists entirely of women, there is still a failure to take up women's issues or involve the rank-and-file in union activities.

Similarly, among tobacco workers of Nipani (discussed by Chhaya Datar elsewhere), where women workers were in the majority, within the union the women accept a division of labour which is based on sexual and educational lines.[40]

This could possibly point to the present structure and mode of functioning of trade unions as institutions and perhaps to the need for an alternative form of organisation itself.

As a women unionist in the U.S. puts it: "Unions ... are organised from the top down with little power emanating from the grassroots. They view this as the best structure to ensure their survival in a business-dominated economy. Unions require their employees to accept the hierarchy and to observe its rules... More insidiously, this top-down centralised framework imposes a particular ideology..."[41]

What seems obvious from the above is that though the trade union is an important organisation for women, women have not been able to, nor can they feel completely at home in it. The union neither exhausts the issues they face nor does it provide the structure to deal with the limited issues it takes up.

The issues trade unions take up are limited at the workplace level. More and more women are being employed in the unorganised sector. Out of these, many are in the form of 'self-employed' workers - ragpickers, vendors, spinners. Those who are not self-employed' like paper-bag makers, chikan workers and many more, work in extremely exploitative conditions and are completely insecure. It is possible that for many of these women, some other forms of organisations like co-operatives would be more appropriate. Again, SEWA has attempted to form co-operatives of hand-block printers, quilt-makers, etc. The set of issues facing these sections is very different -- easy credit facilities, deciding on the product, marketing, etc.

The co-operative alternative is also being tried in big factories, especially where managements have mis-managed or deliberately bled the units. Kamani Tubes in Bombay employing more than 600 workers has been taken over by the workers' co-operative and managed by the co-operative since 1989.[42]

The difficulties inherent in the co-operative model are that however much one would want to democratise one's functioning and work ethically, ultimately one is living, working, buying and selling, in a society where the norms and values are authoritarian and corrupt. How does one draw a line? How does one continue to do the balancing act? These questions, though important to deal with at the level of principles and norms, can often only be really sorted out in practice, in the field, workplace, market. **Reality and women's lives are too complex to insist on a fool-proof solution before trying out newer alternatives.**

At the same time, however, the forces against the self-organising of women and of the other oppressed sections are not only powerful, but also constantly changing their strategies to adapt to the changing situation. Absorption and co-option are important strategies used by these institutions as P.M. Mathew seems to be arguing in his article in this volume. In this article, based on the experience of Kerala, he argues that earlier co-operatives "were viewed as an instrument to arrest the potential upsurge of radical ideas among working class women", while in the post-1975 period they were "an instrument for the greater integration of women into the capitalist system".

It is true that the State and international capital have tried through various means 1) to make use of unorganised female labour to produce for the world market and 2) to contain the militancy and organisation of women workers. Women home-based workers producing electronics goods, women in free trade zones, in small factories excluded from labour legislation have been harnessed for these means. Such ventures have often also enjoyed special benefits because they are supposedly women-oriented.

Even 'local' capitalists like Kirloskars have a women's engineering unit in Pune. This was started about four decades ago as a charitable organisation to provide employment for widows, deserted women, divorcees, etc. The Kirloskars managed to get government concession for these units and the pay-levels were less than half of those of the male workers in the main Kirloskar plant next door, though the production process was almost the same -- lathe machine operations, etc.[43] A more recent example of exploitative capitalist ventures being passed off as women's co-operatives is that of Lijjat papad and Sasa detergent.

It is important to be cautious about ventures like these or schemes which are put forward as women-oriented especially if these ventures and schemes originate from institutions which have shown scant respect for self-organising and employment of women. It is also necessary to delve deeper into the relationships which any of the schemes or organisations initiate or perpetuate, and not remain at the surface reality or at the radical-sounding rhetoric.

At the same time, a rigid attitude of 'unions are good', 'struggle is good', 'co-operatives are bad', etc., would put a spoke in the wheels of women's attempts at trying out newer forms of organisations, newer forms of struggle. This in fact seems to be an unconvincing aspect of P.M. Mathew's arguments.

Ultimately, one may argue, what is the basis of unions themselves? Don't unions accept the labour-capital relationship and evolve strategies which are reactive to capitalist strategies? Yet, unions as organisations of workers have the potentiality to challenge this very basis because workers as a class strive to liberate themselves from the fetters and shackles which imprison them, limit them. Similarly women workers as a section are innovating and attempting to build organisations that address their issues more fully and holistically.

Most forms of organisations which have been developed over the last century have not been able to evolve structures which address themselves to problems of women workers which "stem from the development of new forms of the subordination of women as a gender. Many of these problems present themselves as a series of 'personal', 'individual' difficulties: how to attract a husband or a lover when one has rejected an 'arranged' marriage; how to deal with the contradictions of female sexuality ... how to deal with sexual harassment at work; how to cope with pregnancy, child care and factory work. The concern of women workers with these problems is not a sign that they are 'backward'in consciousness as compared with male workers..."[44]

For women workers, the primacy of gender oppression is a matter of life and death and cannot be postponed till after the struggle against capitalist oppression and exploitation. The forms that workers' organisations have traditionally taken throughout the world have been inadequate from women's point of view because they have failed to recognise and build into their structure the specificity of gender.

New forms of organisation are required that will specifically take up these problems, offering both practical, immediate action on them, and also revealing the social roots of what at first sight appear to be a series of individual personal problems.

REFERENCES

1.   Fernandez Kelly Maria Patricia, *Introduction* in Leacock, Eleanor and Safa Helen and contributors *Women's Work*, Bergin and Garvey Publishers Inc., Massachusetts, U.S.A. 1986, p. 3.

2.   Elson Diane, *Nimble Fingers and Other Fables* in Chapkis Wendy and Enloe Cynthia, *Of Common Cloth*, Transnational Institute, Netherlands, 1983, p. 9.

3.   Ramaswamy Uma, *Women in Organised Industry*, unpublished, 1987, p.3-4.

4.   Jhabvala Renana, *Closing Doors*, Setu Publication, Ahmedabad, 1985.

5.   Savara Mira, *Changing Trends in Women's Employment*, Himalaya Publishing House, Bombay, 1982.

6.   Chhachhi Amrita, *The Case of India*, in Chapkis and Enloe *op.cit.* p. 41.

7.   Elson Diane, *op.cit.*, p. 8.

8.   Savara Mira, *op.cit.*

9.   Gothoskar Sujata, Job *Losses and Closures*, Asia Partnership for Human Development, Hong Kong, 1990.

10.   Chapkis and Enloe, *op.cit.*, p.2.

11.   Committee on the Status of Women, *Towards Equality*, Government of India, New Delhi, 1974.

12.   Elson Diane, *op.cit.*, p.7.

13.   Banerjee Nirmala, *Women and Industrialisation in Developing Countries*, Occasional Paper No. 71, Centre for Studies in Social Sciences, Calcutta, undated.

14.   Gothoskar Sujata, *Declining Employment of Women in the Unionised Sector*, APHD, Hong Kong, 1990.

15.   Gothoskar Sujata, *op.cit.*

16.   Datar Chhaya, *Beedi Workers in Nipani in Sen Ilina, A Space within the Struggle*, Kali for Women, New Delhi, 1990.

17.   Sen Ilina, *Workers' Struggle in Chattisgarh*, in Sen Ilina, *op.cit.*

18.   Kishwar Madhu and Vanita Ruth (Ed.), *In Search of Answers*, Zed Books Ltd., London, 1984.

19.   Kishwar Madhu and Vanita Ruth, *op. cit.*

20.   Gandhi Nandita and Shah Nandita, *Issues at Stake* Kali for Women, New Delhi, 1991.

21.   Gandhi Nandita and Shah Nandita, *op.cit.*

22.   Stree Shakti Sanghatana, *We Were Making History: Life Stories of Women in the Telangana People's Struggle*, Kali for Women, New Delhi, 1989.

23.   Sathe Nirmala, *The Adivasi Struggle in Dhulia*, in Sen Ilina, *op.cit.*

24.   Bahuguna Vimla, *The Chipko Movement*, in Sen Ilina, *op.cit.*

25. Sen Ilina, *Introduction in* Sen Ilina, *op.cit.* p.12.

26. Gothoskar Sujata, *Much more than mere elbow room - Women, work and Law,* NORAD, New Delhi, 1992. '

27. Sen Ilina, *Introduction in Sen Ilina, op.cit. p.12.*

28. Elson Diane and Pearson Ruth, *Third World Manufacturing* in Feminist Review (Ed.), *Waged Work - a reader, Virago Press Ltd., London, 1986.*

29. Gothoskar Sujata, *A Note on Electronic Women Workers in SEEPZ, Bombay,* Women Working Worldwide, London, 1990.

30. Bradley Margaret, *Blue Jeans Blue* in Chapkis and Enloe *op. cit.* p. 89-90.

31. Rohini P H, Sujata S V, and Neelam C, *My Life is One Long Struggle,* Pratishabd Publication, Belgaum, 1983.

32. Elson Diane, *Woman workers, Working woman* in Chapkis and Enloe *op. cit.,* p. 51.

33. Jockes Susan and Baud Isa, *The Double Day* in Chapkis and Enloe, *op.cit.,* p. 59.

34. Sen Ilina, *Introduction,* in Sen Ilina, *op.cit.,* p. 16.

35. Chapkis Wendy, *Using Sex and Satan to Bust the Union* in Chapkis and Enloe, *op. cit.,* p. 107.

36. Elson Diane and Pearson Ruth, *op.cit.,* p. 77.

37. Elson Diane and Pearson Ruth, *op.cit.,* p.78.

38. Rohini P H et al, *op. cit.,* p. 138-9.

39. Geetha, *The Tamil Nadu Construction'workers' Union* in Sen Ilina, *op.cit.,* p.192.

40. Datar Chhaya, *Beedi Workers' in Nipani,* in Sen Ilina, *op.cit.*

41. Rankin Theresa, *Can the Union make Her Strong?,* in Chapkis and Enloe *op. cit.,* p. 100.

42. Gothoskar Sujata, *Kamani Tubes: An Experiment in Workers' Takeover,* Women's Feature Service, New Delhi, 1990.

43. Gothoskar Sujata, *Women in the Informal Sector.* Asia Pacific Development Centre, Kuala Lumpur, 1986.

44. Elson Diane and Pearson Ruth, *op.cit.,* p.89-91.

Chapter 2

Fishworkers' Collective Struggle for Change - The Role of Women

ALEYAMMA VIJAYAN

Background

On the 560 km coast of Kerala live seven lakh fishworkers. Of these, 1,35,000 are active marine fishermen. Until the early 1950s they lived undisturbed by external interventions, adapting and innovating techniques to eke out a living. A consistent emphasis on the part of the Indian Government and international development agencies on the mechanisation of fishing craft led to a spate of projects beginning with the 1950s. Such projects received a boost from developments in the international market for crustaceans - prawns, shrimps, lobsters, etc. 'Trawl nets' which can catch crustaceans living at the bottom of the sea were used. The fisheries sector suddenly became a sector with a large export potential and opportunities for greater profits.

At the hub of the controversy is the mode of fishing pursued by the mechanised trawlers and purse-seiners. The trawler nets sweep the sea-bed and cause destruction of species living at the bottom of the sea as well as juveniles and other plant life. The statistics of the Central Marine and Fisheries Research Institute show that with the advent of trawling in the 1950s, shrimp production of the traditional fisheries diminished drastically. From 1961 to 1970, the total annual shrimp production of the artisanal sector stood at 23,254 tons. Between 1981 and 1985 it crashed to 7,492 tons.

Several factors like the promising US and Japan markets, easy credit from banks, Government subsidies and most importantly the rich prawn grounds of Kerala were responsible for the rapid increase in the number of trawlers. Most of these boats are owned by private entrepreneurs, businessmen and industrialists who corner a large share of the profits by setting up fish processing and export business.

Spontaneous eruption of violent conflicts began in the 1970s as the fishworkers began to experience depletion of marine resources and competition for space in the inshore waters.

The first protests

Violence first erupted on the East coast around Madras as a result of intrusion of trawlers in the inshore waters. Militant struggles also broke out in Goa between the traditional ramponkars and the mechanised trawlers. By 1980, the tensions in Kerala had also intensified and in 1981, the Left Front ministry called for a ban on trawler fishing in June, July and August. This ban was instantly withdrawn for political reasons and this led to violent protests by fishworkers demanding restrictions on destructive fishing by power boats, conservation of fish resources and protection of the interests of small fishworkers.

The Kerala Marine Fishing Regulation Act (1980) and the Kerala Fishermen Welfare Societies Act (1980) were passed by the Government after the struggle had begun. Two commissions were also set up in 1981 and in 1984 to study the problems of fishing and to make appropriate recommendations for improving the conditions. Various measures were suggested to help better conservation and management of the fish resources. In spite of all this, the crisis in the fisheries sector has not been resolved. All the regulatory measures for control of fishing by mechanised boats exist merely on paper and have not been implemented.

Women in the fishing community

Women comprise 49 per cent of the total fishworker population. The labour participation of women in so-called 'gainful' activities is 29.2 per cent. Women contribute a significant share of the household income. In many coastal areas women go and sell the fish, thereby bringing money and other food home to the family. In other areas, they are engaged in other related activities as wage workers in drying, loading and unloading of fish, net-making and other work like coir-making, beedi-making, etc. A substantial number of women work in the prawn-peeling sheds during the prawn season. The above pattern is irrespective of their religious affiliation, although Muslim women in most areas do not go to the market to sell fish.

As fish is a perishable commodity, the work of disposing the catch of fish which is almost invariably women's work takes on an urgency in terms of time and speed. Despite the crucial role women play in the subsistence of the household, they have no decision making power in the community. Most fishing communities are still regulated through a committee of elders or a local panchayat sometimes linked to the religious institution. Women do not have any place on these committees. All the communities have their own ideological justifications for keeping women out of these realms. Taboos relating to women's impurity keep women away from participating as equals in community affairs. Moreover, men expect women to be at their service and in areas where women earn some money, men have no qualms in demanding money even for liquor from their wives, failing which violence against women is not uncommon.

Initial organisational efforts

In the Southern districts of Kerala, non-governmental organisations have been working among fisherwomen since the early 1970s. Village level organisations of women created possibilities for women to get together, express their ideas, and take responsibility in group activities like saving schemes, credit programmes, preventive health programmes, etc. Unlike the fishermen's co-operatives, the emphasis of women's groups was on consciousness-raising programmes and not only on economic activities. Slowly the women were able to see the linkages between their own problems and the larger realities in the country.

Gradually women began to come together. In the initial phases, some of the women spontaneously dropped out because they either felt there were no attractive gains or because they were more reluctant to enter group processes. Some of them found meaning in their collective efforts, where their suppressed talents are given expression and their desire for knowing more and acting on it is satisfied. No matter how small the group is, women do feel the urge to get involved in action and the success of any group depends on its ability to maintain the balance between action, reflection and the group process. This latter relates to the functioning and methods that help members participate and grow. Often an elected committee is formed to handle meetings, to present and discuss issues and to conduct discussions. The process of growth is often slow but perceptible.

In the case of the fisherwomen in Kerala, the initial steps included the taking up of local activities and local issues. Petitioning, organising signature campaigns and going as a group to meet the authorities gave women greater self confidence.

Into wider issues

By 1979, the women were also facing the impact of mechanisation and stiffer competition in markets. They found that markets were flooded with iced fish from distant markets which was sold cheaper than their fresh fish. Their fish, caught by artisanal fishermen, was more expensive because of the diminishing catch. It was possible only for the wealthy merchants with better means of credit and transport to bring in large catches by mechanised means. Women were slowly pushed out or had to face severe competition. The women began to increasingly feel the need to act jointly to take up these issues. They had to walk 10 to 15 kms to reach the market. This meant that they had to walk for atleast 4 to 5 hours in order to sell fish for one hour. Women decided to demand transport facilities to go to the market. The process of empowering women to take up this task took on new dimensions, in which 1) mobilisation was the main task; 2) location of action shifted from the local to the district level; and 3) local political forces had to be contended with.

Mobilisation meant getting other women who were not yet in the local organisations involved in this process. Street theatre was effectively used. Mass petitions and approaching the authorities failed. The authorities offered other welfare measures like creches in coastal villages but were not willing to meet their demand for transport facility which would considerably lessen their ordeal of walking long distances with heavy headloads. Finally the women took to the streets in 1979-80.

Mobilisation for their rights was a new phase of consciousness for the women. This phase brought new experiences, although the struggles had limited success. The women were not granted permission to travel on state public transport vehicles, but the fisheries department organised separate transport for women fish vendors. Although this meant that the stigma about the 'dirty' and 'smelly' fisherwomen could not be effectively challenged then, it was the only possible solution at that time.

A great deal was learnt in this process. How does a demand get represented to the Government? Data has to be collected, the demand has to be clearly stated and the slogans worked out. The organisational details have to be worked out too. Women have to be willing to forfeit work in order to take part in the protests and follow them up, meet the officials, etc. They have also to be ready to collect funds, stick the posters, etc. Women saw how the politicians they had elected to power treated them when they approached them with their demands. They saw how they used the loopholes in the law to wriggle out of any real commitments and they began to see how the entire system was connected. To fight was the only way out, but it would be a long struggle. Such realisation gave them the consciousness of their class position, realising gradually how the interests of the various classes are antagonistic. This made some of the women more militant and willing to take leadership. They became the mainstay of the movement. It is interesting to see how very different personalities come to the forefront, not necessarily women who are concerned with the details, process, etc., as in the earlier phase but women of daring, willing to address the group, willing to rouse other women and give them the confidence to participate, not be hesitant to lead a demonstration and to shout slogans. The same problem of maintaining the balance between action, reflection and process continues to be the crux of the organisational process although the parameters are wider.

The united front

It was this dynamism that women carried into the broader struggle of the fishworkers when in 1981 they participated in a massive protest against trawl fishing. Women were there in the marches, the 'gheraoes', the road and rail blocks, courting arrest and fighting in a militant manner. Although there was some talk about a women's wing within the newly growing fishworkers' union, it was decided that there should be only one union and there was no real need for a separate women's wing either. So although women continued to meet autonomously at the local level, as members of the union, there was only one front and only one platform for discussion.

It was soon very clear that women were as active as the men, or more so in the struggle. But very few women actually came to positions of leadership for obvious reasons that women could not be out late for meetings and due to other related issues.

The women's question

It was during these years, in the early 1980s, that the women's question began to be realised as a question -- a question for the women activists too. Although there was quite a detailed discussion on the issue of the division of male and female roles, it was not earlier understood as to how the ideology of patriarchy was perpetuated to maintain these divisions to the advantage of the men. These divisions were taken as given -- a little more freedom and a little more democracy was what was needed. Questions from other feminist friends like "why don't women go fishing?", "why don't women cycle to the market instead of walking for miles?" were earlier turned down as 'intellectual theorising', 'utopian ideas'. But they gradually became serious questions. It seemed to be true that it was because the men owned the means of production that they exercised a right over women, that too when women contributed substantially to the household income. Why is the entire household the responsibility of the woman when she works for as many hours as the man in an equally strenuous job? What are the roots of the tradition that keep women out of social life in the community; of all the unwritten laws that tell her what she should or should not do, that finally devalue her?

In many ways the growing women's movement around the country stimulated a new thinking process even in the fishworkers' movement. For the first time the problems of the women fish vendors also became the problems of women and mothers. At first the women did not want to talk about their problems considering them private, but it became more and more clear that nothing would change in the private sphere unless it became public and women took these up as their issues too. Wife beating, rape within marriage, all kinds of harassment began to be talked about and women wanted to do something about it all.

Consciousness regarding the women's question also made women aware of the manner in which the fishworkers' union did not really take the question seriously. Besides taking pains to inform the men about the need for taking up such issues, and why the women's question was not detracting from the other working class issues but was an integral part of it, suggestions were also made as to how this could be taken up within the struggle. Two suggestions were made. The first was an organisational suggestion, that is, a way by which women would slowly rise to leadership positions. It was suggested that rotational participation in the committees at the district level should be tried. This was mainly because often for some reason the elected women were not able to participate in all the meetings in which case the women's voice were often not heard. This suggestion could not be carried through because the men said that the women did not put the point across convincingly enough (in retrospect, of course). The second was a question of strategy, that the issues related to women should be taken up as union issues, mainly wife beating and drunkenness leading to violence. Although these were broadly accepted, the men expected that it would be the women who would take up these issues as if the men had nothing to do with such issues.

The urge for autonomy

With greater awareness of the growing atrocities on women, the women in the union felt the urge to respond. In 1986 there was a case of a police riot in a village in Central Kerala. The police had not only looted the village, but also raped women, besides perpetrating other kinds of violence on women whose husbands had deserted the village on hearing that the police were planning to attack. The issue was blown up by the press but the women were initially afraid to testify that they were raped because this would affect them negatively in the future. Some of the women activists from the fishworkers' union went to the spot and invited some of the victims to Trivandrum, the state capital. Discussions were organised with the trade unions in the city and support sought for the village march to the Secretariat. Extensive support was extended to the women and a Commission of Enquiry was instituted. The women's wing of the fishworkers' union was a party to these negotiations and although there was no official women's wing at the time, the banner they spontaneously took up was the Coastal Women's Front.

In 1987 there was a case of murder in one of the coastal villages which was hushed up as suicide. It was the local women's organisation in the village that brought it to light and they were willing to follow it up if some guidance was forthcoming. Again, under the banner of the Coastal Women's Front, a local all party committee was formed and a case was filed; the committee demanded a post-mortem of the buried body. The autopsy findings were that the case was indeed one of a murder.

Later in 1987, the women's front also organised demonstrations to protest against sati and in that year the Women's Day Celebrations were organised jointly by the CPM Mahila Federation and Coastal Women's Front. This conspicuous autonomy that the women's front seemed to exhibit began to be challenged finally by the men in the fishworkers' union. The women seemed to be convinced that it was their right to take up these very important issues. They were forced to do it on their own as the men showed no interest in even discussing them. Moreover the women felt confident that they were able to take an issue to its logical conclusion and without the assistance of the men because it was anyway they who always did the dirty work of running around and organising when any issue had to be taken up. Some of the women felt that the men were reacting because the women were no longer at their beck and call and anyway women's issues should be taken up autonomously.

The solution

So finally the whole question had to be debated and clarified both for the women and for the men. Why was there such a great need for autonomy and what was the best working solution? At this point it must be stated that the male leaders in the union, although visibly distressed by the stand the women had taken, were open to suggestions as to how the women's question could be integrated into the union. But what they wanted were clear cut answers, which of course the women were not in a position to provide, nor did they feel that that was how the issue would find a solution. At the State Convention of the Union, the Chairman of the National Fishermen's Forum had spoken about the 'social movement union' in which a broader understanding of the struggle including the family, social and women's issue would be integrated into the working class struggle. At this State Convention, the only 'vocal' woman State Committee member confronted the gathering about their lip service to the women's question saying that women were even refused membership in some districts of the state. She emphasised the fact that unless the men took time to study the issue, to see it in the social context and to analyse it, they would not be able to understand it. Somehow she got the State Committee to take decisions on at least taking special efforts to see that some seminars would be conducted first on this subject and that special interest would be taken in attending to issues relating to women at local levels.

Subsequently from early 1988, efforts have begun on these lines. It was finally decided at the district level (one district) that there would be a women's committee with autonomy within the union. This committee could coopt women who would support them. If would be chaired by an elected woman member, who would have the freedom to decide on issues they wanted to take up, to determine their own plan of action and propose it to the larger district committee. But these decisions were taken after a long process of discussion and analysis. Efforts were made to build in the women's question into the broader analysis of society showing how patriarchy, like class and caste, penetrates all areas of life.

This autonomous committee within the larger union has only just started functioning and only the future can tell how effective it would be.

Foreseeable inherent difficulties

Developing a feminist perspective within a trade union is no simple task, nor is it easy to sustain participation and leadership of women in union activities. Developing a feminist perspective is a long process and is not possible if there are only structural changes within the union.

Structural changes are the first step but then if structural changes have to be effective many other changes have also to be initiated. For instance, simple things like seeing that meetings are organised at a time when women can attend them. Even if this takes place, then who would look after the children at home or who would cook the food if the women are expected to be out for a fairly long time. And there are numerous such examples. The perspective is built up only if women constantly participate and are vocal in carrying decisions through. This is still a long way off. If women are given no voice in any other social forum, then it takes quite a while before they can be comfortable with themselves and participate in the union confidently. It is moreover very difficult for men to develop the patience that gives women the time and space to develop their own thinking on issues which have rarely been discussed. The men want everything clear and properly thought out not realising that they too have to contribute to the thinking process. Then the taking up of women's issues itself is a long and painstaking process because they involve not only factual issues but a great deal of beliefs, psychological barriers, accepted norms and taboos that have to be questioned.

Sustaining women's participation in leadership and in the daily run of things is also not an easy task. Finally all the household burden falls on the women. It is impossible for women to go out to work, attend to all unforseen happenings in the home like sickness, family problems etc., and then still have time for organisational work. Some women go on by their sheer will to do something but then how are these women helped to grow? They are good at the level of action, mobilising and on this front they are leaders but then how do they carry an argument through? How do they build up a wider understanding of problems? They are too tired to concentrate at sessions and to follow any logical arguments. How do such women then convince the men who want to have everything clearly thought out if they have to ratify it?

So while concluding that there has been a marked evolution in understanding the women's question in the fishworkers' union, only the future will tell how this actually helps to develop a feminist perspective in struggle.

Chapter 3

Struggle for Equal Rights for Women Contract Workers of Ennore Thermal Power Station

Priya

Introduction

O n the Ist of April 1985, seventeen slag workers working for the contractor Husain Sharif at the Ennore Thermal Power Station (ETPS) were involved in an accident. Of the seventeen workers, seven women succumbed to fatal burn injuries and nine others were severely injured. The workers had just finished their usual work of loading the lorries with the hot cinder waste. As it was raining they took shelter under the ash-pump house where they generally had their noon meal. Usually, hot slag from the boiler falls through a pipe running under the ash-pump house into the cooling system from which it is collected by the workers and loaded into the waiting lorries. On this day, a shower of boiling hot cinder-ash descended on the workers instead of falling into the cooling system, killing seven women and severely injuring the others.

The next day all the papers carried the news. Two Pennurimai Iyakkam activists went to the spot for investigation. Pennurimai Iyakkam is a women's organisation which for the past 8 years has been involved in struggles against exploitation of woman in many forms - against bride-burning, demanding maintenance for women, combatting police harassment of women, and other issues. As our members are mostly from the lower socio-economic section we have also had to grapple with issues like housing and amenities for the urban poor.

The activists met the injured who were being treated at the Stanley Medical Hospital and the families of the 7 women who had died. They found out some shocking facts about the working of the contract labour system. Ennore is an industrial area within a large slum. The population here comprises a number of Burmese repatriates, Adidravidars, Harijans, etc. Most of the workers, especially the contract workers working in the factories in the area come from nearby slums. Most of the contract workers in the Ennore Thermal Power Station (ETPS) too come from these slums known as Annai Sivagami Nagar, Burma Nagar and the neighbouring Minjur area. There is a high degree of pollution of both air and water, and many of the poorer residents of the area suffer from tuberculosis due to the coal dust prevalent in the air.

The ETPS plant is under the control of the Tamil Nadu Electricity Board (TNEB) which is a department of the State Government. Pennurimai Iyakkam's investigation revealed the true story of what happened on 1st April 1985. The entire accident seemed to have taken place purely due to the negligence of the ETPS authorities. Due to a lack of any other facilities, women contract workers had to take shelter under the ash-pump house near the boiler pipe. No supervisor had advised them of the danger of standing there. Every day they had their usual noon meal in the same place, that is, under the ash-pump house. When the accident occurred on the 1st of April 1985, neither the Junior Engineer nor the Assistant Engineer lent any assistance to the workers. No ambulance was called for these severely injured contract workers which is the general practice when a regular employee is affected. No first-aid was given. Some of the co-workers took the injured and admitted them in the Stanley Medical Hospital. The contractor was also summoned by them. Had the injured been admitted to the Kilpauk Medical Hospital where there is a separate department for the treatment of burns, probably some of the deaths could have been averted.

Conditions of the Contract Workers in ETPS

This industrial accident in the Ennore Thermal Power Station just outside Madras led us at Pennurimai Iyakkam to begin working with contract workers. Though we were mainly instrumental in organising the women contract workers, our demands were placed in the general context of regularising contract workers as a whole. This is because we see the question of exploitation of women belonging to the lower socio-economic strata as part of the general social repression of the entire class.

Pennurimai Iyakkam activists found that one of the biggest violators of the Contract Labour Act was this State undertaking. The workers were treated like sub-humans and had to work for 8 hours without lunch or tea-breaks. They were denied access to the canteens. The women slag workers were paid only Rs. 7/- a day. There were no rest rooms or washing facilities provided. When the TNEB officials visited the plant, the workers were asked to hide themselves from view as groups of workers standing about or eating made factory premises look unsightly. Sometimes the women were asked to work in the Assistant Engineer's house on the promise that they would not be laid off if they did so. All safety regulations were violated by the management of this public sector undertaking. New recruits from among the contract workers were made to work on dangerous operations like crushing coal on the conveyor belt. Young boys were even made to move under the belt and remove any obstacles to its smooth movement. The only "supervisors" were the co-workers. Most of them were unaware of the dangerous nature of the operations they were asked to perform. Small wonder then, that accidents among contract workers were a frequent occurrence at the ETPS. Apart from lack of provision of in-house training to workers, no safety clothing like gumboots, goggles, asbestos suits, etc. were provided. The Junior Engineer sat in the control room and 'oversaw' the entire operation from there. This actually isolated him from activities going on in the factory. The contractor generally employed about two supervisors in his pay but they would be more in the nature of slave-drivers than skilled foremen.

The most shocking truth revealed by our investigation was that the contract labour system as a whole provided for most of the unskilled labour supply in the plant. Even some secretarial work like typing was done by the contract workers. In the ETPS there was a clear distinction between contract workers and regular employees. All skilled workers were regular and held certain definite jobs, though some of these were also occasionally performed by contract workers. A few women were employed as regular employees for jobs like sweeping and chemical analysis. There were about 500 women contract workers. They were denied maternity benefits, sick leave with pay which even contract workers are entitled to, precisely because they were ignorant of their rights. Medical and other benefits under the ESI Act were not extended to the contract workers by the ETPS Management. In fact ETPS was one of the biggest violators of the Act.

Involvement of Pennurimai Iyakkam: Representation and Formulation of Demands

The gruesome accident had been widely covered by the press. In order to avoid embarrassment the State Government announced in the legislature on 4th April 1985 that Rs.500/- would be given as compensation to the injured and Rs.2000/- would be given to the families of those who had lost their lives. This fell far short of the Rs. 10,000/ announced as compensation for families of victims of accidents resulting in the course of their employment to be allotted from the Chief Minister's relief fund. This had earlier been announced as a Government order. It applied however, only to regular employees. We decided that the compensation announced for the families of the accident victims in ETPS accident was too small, especially in view of the fact that the accident would not have occurred but for the gross negligence of the ETPS officials.

By May 1985 however, even this meagre ex-gratia payment had not been given. It was clear that this was just a ruse staged by the State Government to gag the mouths of the critics. Representations were made by the families of the accident victims. Pennurimai Iyakkam sent a petition to the Electricity Minister, the chairman of the TNEB and the Labour Secretary which included the following demands.

1. Compensation to the families of the workers who had lost their lives and those who were injured should be increased to Rs.10,000/- and Rs.1000/ respectively.
2. Compensation as per section 9-A of the Workmen's Compensation Act should be deposited with the Commissioner of Labour for each accident victim.
3. Safety measures as per the Factories Act should be instituted to prevent the occurrence of further accidents.
4. The Abolition and Regulation of Contract Labour Act,

    dealing with rest room, canteen, creche, etc, should be implemented.

5.   Minimum wages for workers of Thermal Power Stations should be introduced in the schedule to the Minimum Wages Act and implemented.

6.   Officials responsible for the accident should be prosecuted.

7.   Unnecessary reduction in the labour force should be checked and wages should be paid during forced lay-offs.

The seventh demand revealed a very pertinent question in ETPS labour-management relations. Contract workers were laid-off when a particular unit was working below par. Workers however had to present themselves every day at the factory-gates in the hope of getting work. They therefore wasted a whole day waiting without any wages.

Another anti-labour activity is the practice of giving tenders to the person bidding lower than even the estimated cost. The system of employment of contract labour worked in this manner : a tender was issued to the public and an auction of contractors was held. Contractors were of two types: contractors responsible only for supplying labour, and contractors responsible for the work as well as for supplying labour. The lowest bids were accepted. However, this system was so corrupt and competitive that the contractors often bid lower than the estimated cost so that in work contracts, workers were paid very low wages (Rs. 7/- to Rs. 7.50/- per day).

To lend weight to our demands, a signature campaign was also conducted and 500 signatures from the general public were collected and presented to the Secretary of the Department of Public Works. This highlighted the fact that the accident would not have occurred but for the fact that the slag workers had to take shelter from the rain near a boiler. The area was cordoned off and a "Danger" sign put up only after the accident.

Neither the compensation under the Workmen's Compensation Act nor the ex-gratia payment as per the State Government announcement was given to the injured workers or to the families of the workers who were killed. Pennurimai Iyakkam sent a representative to New Delhi to meet the Secretary of the Labour Department.Talks between them ranged from the question of non-payment of compensation to the affected families to regularisation of the contract workers of the ETPS.

However, the result was only a mild letter by the Labour Secretary to the Chairman of the TNEB enquiring into what measures had been taken to curb the contract labour system. A surprising fact that came to light during our meetings with officials in the Ministry of Labour was that there was no documentation regarding the Thermal Power Station. Cases were not filed for compensation under the Workmen's Compensation Act even for the dependents of the seven women who had died in the accident.

Meanwhile the women workers had been organised into committees for each unit in the plant and regular meetings were held at which Pennurimai Iyakkam activists would also be present.

Repression Begins

The local power interests represented by the contractors and sub-contractors resented the unification of the hitherto scattered contract workers. They began to issue subtle threats to those who took the lead. A gate meeting was held deploring the anti-labour activities of the contractor and the ETPS management backed by the TNEB. For the first time contract workers took an active part in a demonstration and shouted slogans against the ETPS authorities. Soon after, one woman worker and another factory-level activist working as a sweeper in the civil section were threatened inside the factory gates by a contractor. A sub-contractor who helped Pennurimai Iyakkam organise the workers, was boycotted by other contractors and the workers of the contractors were not assigned to him and he was threatened with physical harm by the same 'gang'. Representations were made to the Police Commissioner and eyewitnesses were also taken to meet him but to no avail. Meanwhile the promised compensation deposited with the Labour Commissioner for each affected family was handed over to them, but not before a writ for dispensation of the amount had been filed in the High Court and won. We also learned that a sub-committee had been constituted to go into the system of contract labour in TNEB.

Hitherto, the trade unions organising regular employees at the ETPS had not taken any cognizance of the problems of the contract workers even though the accidents among contract labourers were an every day occurrence at the site and they had other numerous grievances. Now that some organisation had entered the fray on behalf of the workers, and a women's organisation at that, other unions began to take an interest in the workers.

The ETPS management realised that women workers had been organised into an active and questioning body. They decided to cut out dissidence by preventing women from being employed on the premises of the factory.

In August 1985, when the tender for work and labour was reissued to the public, it contained a specific provision that no women were to be employed and in several places the words 'only men' were specifically used. This arbitrary decision by the ETPS Management was in no way communicated to the four hundred women who worked in the plant unloading coal, feeding crushers, working on parts under construction and doing all the sweeping, the cleaning and dusting off of the coal dust from the machinery. A writ was filed in the High Court by 29 women that wearing a saree would not be an impediment for movement at work. The High Court directed the re-employment of women as their exclusion was discriminatory and unnecessary. However, the court's order delivered on the 23rd of August, 1985 was not implemented till the 7th of September, 1985.

By this time a non-party based union had began to organise the workers. Immediately workers in the civil section were threatened with compulsory lay-off. Another case was filed by 200 contract workers and the ETPS Management gave a guarantee in court that even if contractors were changed the present workers would not be terminated.

The ETPS Management has now announced a new scheme in the form of co-operative society for all workers including contract workers. This is supposed to guarantee to the workers minimum wages, Provided Fund, etc. Obviously this is nothing but 'a ploy to keep workers happy' because workers are being made aware about their legal rights and about the abuses of the contract labour system. Immediately after this, another major accident took place when Jayavelu, a migrant worker from Dharmapuri district died of electrocution from a high tension cable due to the negligence of the factory authorities. When the union conducted dharanas protesting against this accident, reprisals from the management immediately followed in the form of physical threats and refusal to allow the union and Pennurimai Iyakkam members to join the co-operative society. The struggle continues.

The most positive contribution by Pennurimai Iayakkam to the struggle of the ETPS contract workers was the effort made to break the fear psychosis among the workers and the build up their sense of solidarity so that the workers are now able to face any repression from the management or the contractors without flinching. Pennurimai Iyakkam has now also started organising the workers at the community level so that there is an all-round building up of the worker's strength.

Chapter 4

Women's Struggles in the Informal Sector: Two Case Studies from SEWA

Renana Jhabvala

Introduction

There has been, in the literature on the informal sector, a great deal of debate on what exactly constitutes this sector. Here we do not go into this debate, but instead we attempt to identify who are the workers of the informal sector. The informal sector, as we see it, extends to all sectors of the economy. It is rural and urban, in the forests and on the mountains, in plantations and in mines and in all other sectors where work is done. The workers of the informal sector can be divided into three categories:

1. Vendors and hawkers: who hawk goods such as vegetables, fruits, fish, eggs, garments etc.
2. Homebased producers: making products such as beedis, agarbattis, garments, cloth, small furniture, footwear, gold products, handicrafts, etc.
3. Labourers: who sell their labour such as agricultural labour, construction labour, stone breakers, etc.

About 89% of all employment is generated in the informal sector. Unofficially (there being no official estimates) estimates suggest that 40% of this sector comprises of women workers.

There have been isolated attempts to organise these workers, giving rise to some vendors' unions, associations of agricultural labourers, co-operatives of handloom weavers and the like. However, except in a few cases women usually get left out of these organising attempts.

This paper attempts to describe an experiment in organising women in the informal sector. Self Employed Women's Association (SEWA) was registered as a trade union of self-employed women in 1972. The word "self-employed" was deliberately preferred to informal or unorganised as it conferred dignity on the worker. Since then, SEWA has organised women both in rural and urban areas and has a membership of about 25,000 women.

SEWA has adopted the twin strategies of struggle and development. Struggle carried out mainly through the union takes the form of fighting for one's rights. Development takes the form of building alternative economic structures such as co-operatives. Here we will discuss some struggles as carried out by the union.

SEWA's Struggle

SEWA believes that struggle is an essential part of development. In the process of development, there are many cases when injustice has to be effectively opposed, struggled against. When a policeman beats and kicks a helpless fruit vendor, he has to be opposed. When an employer makes garment stitchers labour for ten hours a day and they earn only Rs. 3/-, a struggle has to be launched. When the government refuses to give medical treatment to beedi workers from a clinic that is especially opened for them, a protest must be launched. When a cart-puller breaks her leg in a street accident, someone must be held liable.

SEWA's experience has shown that injustice exists at three levels. First is the face of injustice that women directly see—the direct exploiter. This may take the form of a cruel policeman, hardhearted employer or a vicious contractor. Supporting the direct exploiter however is the second level of injustice - the government agencies and the legal structure. The Labour Department, for example, which is meant to protect the workers has become corrupted by the employers and often helps the employer to get around the law. The Municipality treats the poor vendor as a criminal. The courts take years to give final judgments and these judgments are usually not in favour of the poor, especially if they are women.

All this exploitation can be sustained because of the injustice at the highest level - at the level of policies and laws. When our cities and towns are planned, no space is given to vending so that the vendors are doomed to always remain "illegal". Labour laws are conceived with the organised sector in mind so that there is no protection for the homebased garment worker. The Police Acts treat the poor and the homeless as criminals.

SEWA has found that in order to be effective, struggle has to be carried out at all three levels of injustice. First, through direct action - meeting with and writing to the employers or the police. Morchas, demonstrations, satyagrahas and strikes are the most effective forms of direct action. Second, SEWA deals with government departments through complaints and uses the legal structure by filing cases in court. Finally SEWA tries to bring about policy changes - to change the concepts of town planning, to make labour laws more responsive to the self-employed sector, to make the insurance companies aware of the problems of the self employed. But action - whether direct or indirect, legal or policy - is useful only if it leads to another phase of organising. The most used motto of SEWA unions is : "Organise, organise, organise."

But why is it necessary to organise? Basically, because SEWA is only a representative of the self-employed women and unless the self employed are organised they cannot agree on common issues, common actions, common ideologies. To organise means to bring people together, to think through their common problems, to agree on their common issues, to decide on common action and to forge a common ideology.

However, organising these women, who are often the poorest of the poor, is not easy. There are strong vested interests which do not wish to see them united and which try to defeat all organising attempts. At the same time generations of oppression, both as workers and as women have bred complexes in women which make their coming together very difficult. What are some of the problems that SEWA faces in organising? The most pervasive one is the very real fear of losing whatever small income they might now have. Usually an employer or other exploiter reacts to organising by harsh measures such as dismissal or arrest. *The harshest treatment is reserved for the neediest and poorest women, who are the most defenceless. So those who would really benefit from organising are the most fearful of doing so.*

There are also a lot of *divisions among workers* which prevent them from coming together. These are generally the divisions of community, caste, religion or region. Another problem particular to women is that they have *difficulty in identifying themselves as workers,* although they may be employed in income generating activity 10 hours a day. Since they see themselves primarily as housewives, mothers and wives, they find it difficult to identify with each other on common work issues. Yet another difficulty is that they are often *unaware of the laws* meant to protect them and the agencies meant to help them.

Inspite of all these problems women workers do organise and do struggle. None of the problems are insurmountable and the women exhibit a rare degree of courage and ability to bear suffering. And once they become accustomed to the idea of themselves as workers, they begin to show a lot of fellow feeling both as workers and as women.

Perhaps one of the secrets to organising is "*to keep on keeping on*". No *one* action ever leads to success. *No failure is permanent.* Organising is a series of ups and downs. Often when you have almost given up, a new factor or a timely event will lead to success. Success is rarely absolute, and is often only a compromise. Yet a compromise position is the launching pad for another action forward. One issue often leads to another or a series of issues, each more important, more basic than the last. And so SEWA just keeps on organising.

I would like to illustrate SEWA's organising method by giving two detailed examples, that of vendors and of beedi workers. Of course, each struggle has its own peculiarities, its own pattern and trend, but the two examples should offer an insight into how each of the strategies of direct action, government and legal action and policy action is used.

THE VENDORS' UNION

Chandaben first came to SEWA to ask for help is getting a bank loan. Later she brought her two sisters-in-law also for bank loans. Soon she was a regular visitor at the SEWA office. Sometimes she would bring neighbours, friends and relatives for loans; at other times she would just drop in because she liked the atmosphere at SEWA. Before long, Chandaben and Elaben became friends and Chandaben began talking about her problems.

She is an old-clothes' seller. Every afternoon she walks about the middle-class colonies with a basket full of new pots and pans. She exchanges these pots for people's old clothes. In the evening she and her husband repair these clothes to make them look as good as new and the next morning she sells them in the old-clothes' market.

Police and the old-clothes' sellers

Chandaben is a Vaghari, one of the backward castes. The main problem of her community is that they are commonly perceived as thieves. Because of this undeserved reputation the police are constantly harassing the old-clothes' vendors. Whenever the police felt like it they would arrest a Vaghari man or, less commonly, woman on a charge of theft. They would take him to the police station and beat him till he "confessed" to a theft. The real reason, however, is extortion. The police, insist that the vendor pays a bribe often up to Rs. 1,000, before being released. The whole Vaghari community was terrified of the police, their beating and their extortions.

The situation came to a head one night at 11 P.M. when Elaben received a phone call. It was Chandaben. The police had picked up her nephew, Raju on a charge of theft. But her nephew could not possibly have been guilty because he had been in the hospital for an appendicitis operation all the week before. Chandaben was afraid that in his weakened condition Raju would not be able to withstand the customary police beatings. Something had to be done fast.

So Elaben rushed to the police station. A big crowd of old-clothes' vendors was outside the gate. Chandaben and her sister were inside waiting for Elaben. They were allowed to meet Raju who was lying on the floor obviously still very weak. But fortunately, the beating had not yet begun.

Elaben and Chandaben sought the Police Inspector In-charge of the station. Elaben pleaded with him to release the boy. She personally guaranteed his innocence. The Police Inspector was surprised to see a well-dressed woman pleading for a Vaghari in the middle of the night.

From his window he could see the crowd of about 70 old-clothes' sellers, who had come with Elaben. He asked Raju to be brought before him. Raju was brought and lifted up his shirt to show his fresh appendectomy scar. The Police Inspector then ordered Raju to be released. "I am doing this just because, you, a respectable person, have come to me", he told Elaben, "This is the first time I have released a Vaghari without getting a confession of theft from him. These Vagharis are all .hieves."

The old-clothes sellers were jubilant. This was the first time one of them had been released without being beaten, and it showed that their lot was not entirely hepeless. They *could* fight police harassment. This first successful attempt set the pattern for challenging police high-handedness. As word of this success got around the old-clothes-seller communities, they began besieging Chandaben to intervene whenever the police arrested any of them on the usual theft charges. Chandaben would honestly investigate and determine whether the person arrested was really innocent. If she felt he was, she would come to SEWA and Elaben would send one of the organisers to the police station. At the same time a crowd of old-clothes-sellers would gather outside the police station. Because of the crowd outside, the police would feel restrained in beating up the person arrested. The organiser and Chandaben would meet the Police Inspector In-Charge to vouch for the suspect's innocence.

Once a woman, Pannaben, was arrested in the market while selling old clothes. The policemen pulled an expensive sari out of her basket and said she had stolen it. The Police Inspector Incharge would not release Pannaben even on the SEWA organiser's request. He too said the sari was stolen. Pannaben insisted that she had exchanged the sari for pots with a lady in Navrangpura, a posh area. So the SEWA organiser, Neeruben, and Chandaben went to the address where Pannaben said she had exchanged the sari. They met the lady of the house who confirmed that she had indeed exchanged a sari with Pannaben. Neeruben was able to persuade her to come to the police station and identify the sari in the presence of the Police Inspector. Only after this lady's evidence was Pannaben released.

Old-clothes sellers' association

Soon Chandaben developed into a real leader. Other old-clothes sellers came to her whenever they had a problem. She was elected vice-president of SEWA. "She has a fire within", Elaben says.

Chandaben and some male old-clothes-sellers decided to form an old-clothes-sellers' association. SEWA, while not directly involved with this association, extended full support to it. The Association felt that many of their problems arose because of the common perception of

Vagharies as thieves. They decided they should try and combat this perception. Once a popular Gujarati magazine published an article about old-clothes-sellers in which someone was quoted as saying that these people were generally thieves. The association decided to protest. They marched through the city telling the common people how they had been defamed. Then they marched to the magazine's office. They also filed a case of defamation in the Civil Court.

The vegetable vendors

Like Chandaben, Maniben, a vegetable seller, also first came to SEWA to get a loan. She came back many times and began talking about vegetable vendors. One day she said to Neeruben, "You have been doing so much for old-clothes-vendors, why not do something for us." Neeruben had been in touch with the Government workers' education department which wanted to organise a class for women vendors. So SEWA organised a workers' education class for vegetable vendors, teaching them simple accounting procedures to supplement their sharp intuitive calculating abilities. In this class the Vaghari vendors complained that they too were harassed by the police. They were beaten with lathis, their baskets were kicked into the ditch and sometimes they were arrested. The worst affected were the women who sat in Manekchowk. Of these women, the most vocal was Laxmiben.

Manekchowk is the main fruit and vegetable market of Ahmedabad city. The vendors and hawkers have been selling in Manekchowk square for the last three generations from mother to daughter or father to son. Over half of the vendors are women. However, as the city grows, the square gets more and more crowded, and pedestrians, cars, bicycles, rickshaws, handcarts and vendors jostle each other for the limited space.

One day Laxmiben came to the SEWA office with the news that a young woman, Rajiben, had been arrested. Neeruben accompanied Laxmiben to the police station. The visit to the police station made Neeruben realise that the problem at Manekchowk is quite different from that of the old-clothes-sellers. The vendors were arrested not for theft but for 'encroachment'. According to the Bombay Police Act, the vendors were encroaching on traffic space and could be fined by the police. Under the Act, the accused vendor must pay the fine to the traffic court, otherwise she would be sent a summons. If she did not obey the summons she would be sent an arrest warrant. Rajiben had been arrested under this Bombay Police Act and therefore could only be bailed out the next day when the courts opened. Rajiben had to spend the night in jail.

But Laxmiben said that the real reason Rajiben was in jail was her refusal to pay bribes to the policemen on duty. The vegetable vendors could not 'legally' vend in Manekchowk because they had not been given hawkers' licences by the Ahmedabad Municipality. So they could be 'removed' any time. The policemen on duty used this illegal status of the vendors to extort bribes. If they did not pay, the policemen would beat them and kick their wares. The police would also fine them and then not give them the notice. Rajiben did not even know that a summons was out in her name because the policeman didn't give it to her. He wanted to drive home this point by making her spend the night in jail. Later SEWA found out that this particular policeman was running a restaurant in his off-duty hours with the vegetables, fruit and fish that he extorted from the vendors!

Some policemen were habitual sadists. They enjoyed beating the vendors, especially women and children. If a vendor objected to this treatment, she or he could be arrested under charges of obstructing a policeman in execution of his duty! One Police Inspector used to come on a motorbike and run his motorbike onto the vendors' baskets.

The police persecution of the vendors was encouraged by the big shopkeepers. Manekchowk has a "pukka" market where the shopkeepers sell fruit and vegetables from stalls. They complain that vendors set up shop just outside their pukka market, selling the same fruits and vegetables and under-cutting their prices. The shopkeepers would write to the police department complaining that vendors created public nuisance. They also bribed individual policemen to harass the vendors.

The Municipal officers too would collect their "hafta" (weekly payment) from the vendors. If a vendor did not pay, the Municipal anti-encroachment van would appear and her basket would be dumped into it. Later SEWA found out that this was permissible under the Bombay Municipal Act. Occasionally the Municipality would have a 'clear up' drive and the anti-encroachment van would come and take away all the vendors' baskets. Not only would the vendor lose her days' earnings but the capital invested in the vegetables and the basket as well.

Licenses for vendors

The day after Rajiben was released, Elaben called a meeting of Manekchowk vendors in the SEWA office. What could SEWA do? After much discussion it was decided that since the root of the problem was the vendors' illegal status, SEWA should try to get licences for the vendors. At the same time SEWA should complain to the authorities against police brutality.

Laxmiben and Neeruben collected a list of women vendors in Manekchowk and applied to the Municipality for licences in their names. When there was no answer from the Municipality, SEWA sent a reminder and one was sent every six months, but to this day the Municipality has not replied.

Meanwhile Neeruben went a number of times with Laxmiben and Rajiben to complain to the Police Inspector In-charge of Manekchowk area about the constables' high-handedness. Elaben also met the Police Commissioner. The result of all these efforts was that police behaviour towards the vendors did improve.

However, such small mercies were not long lasting. Police officials must move on. Whenever a constable, a Police Officer or a Police Commissioner was transferred, the cycle of beatings began all over again and a new relationship had to be established with the new men.

Protest

In 1977, there was a new State government which ordered wholesale transfers in the police department. The new policemen were particularly brutal. In the summer of 1978, SEWA had a meeting of vendors and it was decided to hold a protest demonstration - appropriately on Independence Day, August 15. A thousand vendors gathered and the procession wound its way around the city, ending up in a meeting at Parade Ground. The procession went past the police stations and the vendors loudly shouted slogans outside each one. The procession ended in a meeting addressed by the Chief Minister. The Police Commissioner and Municipal Commissioner were also invited. Although the Chief Minister later proved to be very helpful, at the meeting he told the vendors "Why do you leave your villages to come to the cities? You should all return where you came from."

The old-clothes-vendors also participated in the procession which marked a turning point for the vendors. Since 1978 there have been practically no arrests of old-clothes vendors for theft. It also made an impression on the Municipal Commissioner who agreed to meet with Elaben to help the vendors of Manekchowk. Elaben told the Municipal Commissioner that the vendors should somehow be legalised, but the Commissioner refused them licences. He argued that if he gave licences to these, then the 50,000 other vendors of Ahmedabad would also claim licences. He also said that the Municipality might want to use the space for something else and if the vendors were licensed it would be impossible to move them out. Finally the Municipal Commissioner agreed to 'regularise' the vendors by drawing lines on the pavement to mark their spots. The Municipality agreed to recognise these spaces as valid vending spots and the vendors agreed to stay within the limits drawn by the Municipality.

The regularisation gave the vendors the courage to stop giving bribes to the policemen. Laxmiben was the first to stop her weekly tip to the constables and she urged the others to follow suit. The constable was very angry with Laxmiben but he dared not beat her, so he filed 15 cases against her. However, Laxmiben with Manulben, SEWA's organiser, appeared in the traffic court and pleaded her case before the magistrate. The magistrate let her off with fine of Rs 5/-.

However, the forces against the vendors were too strong. The traffic police were unhappy about the increasing congestion as was the Municipality. The shopkeepers were keen to get rid of the vendors too. The situation finally came to a head in 1980. A man died in a fight between two rival groups. The police declared a curfew and Manekchowk was closed to vendors, shopkeepers, pedestrians and traffic alike. However, the police decided that this was an opportune time to get rid of the vendors, and when the curfew was lifted, the vendors were prohibited from going back to their assigned spots.

Satyagraha

Laxmiben, Rajiben and a group of other vendors came to the SEWA office in great agitation. If the police didn't allow them to vend in Manekchowk, where would they go? How would they earn? They had been sitting there for three generations. Surely they had a right to be there. Elaben phoned the Police Commissioner, who said it was the Municipality's decision not to allow vendors to sit. So the next day,

Elaben, Laxmiben and two others went to see the Municipal Commissioner. He said it wasn't his decision but that of the police. Again Elaben rang up the Police Commissioner. Now the Police Commissioner was not available. Every time Elaben called, the Police Commissioner would be out. This went on for a few days. But the vendors came to the SEWA office in despair every day.

Finally, Elaben and Laxmiben took a group of about 20 vendors and three SEWA organisers to the Police Commissioner's office. As usual, the Commissioner was 'out'. "Then, we'll wait here till he comes", Elaben declared. So the vendors camped out in the gardens while Elaben and the organisers took turns in the waiting room. Four hours later, the Police Commissioner relented and met his visitors.

"The Police Commissioner was in a rage", Elaben recalls, "He said the vendors were causing nuisance in Manekchowk and were becoming a law and order problem. I pointed out that the vendors were not responsible for the disturbances and should not be punished. Finally, the Commissioner calmed down and promised to 'see' if he could accommodate the vendors."

Still the police did not allow the vendors to sit. For five days the vendors would have a meeting in SEWA and decide to wait an extra day. On the sixth day they became impatient. Most had no other source of income and with two weeks without work they were down to one meal a day of dry roti and chillies. Others had begun to pawn jewellery and even their dishes. So again a delegation went to meet the Police Commissioner and again he said he would 'see'. Elaben and the vendors concluded he was not sincere.

A meeting of all 350 vendors was called in the big TLA meeting hall and Laxmiben explained the attitude of the Police Commissioner. What was to be done? All the vendors felt very strongly about it. "If they make us leave Manekchowk, they might as well kill us," said Laxmiben, "it will be better than the slow death of starvation." "Are you ready to brave the police and claim what is yours?" asked Elaben. All hands went up. The vendors were ready for action.!

It was the 28th of January. It was decided that the vendors should occupy their rightful places two day later. The thirtieth of January was Gandhiji's death anniversary. In a fitting tribute to Gandhiji, it would be a satyagraha.

Elaben told Mr. Buch, then president of SEWA, of this decision. He was not happy about this direct confrontation and tried to dissuade her. But Elaben was firm. Then she informed the Police Commissioner and the Municipal Commissioner. The Police Commissioner was angry. He phoned Mr. Buch and told him to 'control' Elaben. He said he would restore the vendors in his own way. But Elaben said the vendors had lost faith in the Police Commissioner's promises and if no action was taken now, they would lose their place forever. Finally Mr. Buch agreed.

Mr Barot, an influential secretary in TLA was also against the proposed satyagraha. The reason was his political affiliations. Mr. Barot had joined the ruling Janata Party and was the Labour Minister. Mr. Barot was unwilling to have any action which could be construed as "anti-government."

Laxmiben and a few of the other vendors reached Manekchowk at 7 a.m. on 30th morning. By 8 a.m. most of the vendors and all SEWA organisers were there. The shopkeepers curiously watched. No policeman was in sight yet. SEWA had already planned out the strategy - all the vendors were to sit against the wall in their usual places with their baskets.

SEWA organisers were to stand among them. If arrested, no one was to panic but to quietly go into the police vans. Some of the vendors were timid and huddled in a corner refusing to sit in their places; Laxmiben, Rajiben and others urged them on. Soon all the vendors were sitting with their baskets and the organisers stood by their side. The baskets were empty because the vendors did not want to risk losing vegetables in case there was a disturbance.

At 9 a.m. the police vans began arriving, one after another. Five of them stood at one end of the market and policemen poured out. They seemed as uncertain as SEWA about what would happen next. But as the police arrived, passers-by began to collect and soon there was a crowd of people pushing and jostling. Goondas began shouting abuse at the vendors and the vendors shouted back. Some vendors got up to get closer and fight with the goondas. SEWA organisers kept trying to make the vendors visit down and keep quiet. The policemen walked up and down as if to check the law and order problem, but wherever a posse of policemen walked, a crowd would gather and there would be chaos. The police strategy seemed to be to create a disturbance so that then they would treat it as a "law and order" problem and "pick-up" the vendors.

Then the shopkeepers got into the act. They began shouting. "The vendors are ruining our business; if they can sit on the pavement, so can we." And shoving some vendors aside, shopkeepers sat on the pavement with baskets in front of them! They looked so funny sitting there crosslegged in the street in their tight pants and clean white shirts. They too were trying to create a disturbance - sometimes sitting, sometimes jumping up and down, shouting and appealing to the passers-by and gathering a crowd. The vendors became more and more excitable and would respond to every provocation, shouting and rushing up from their places. The SEWA organisers kept trying to calm down the vendors and at the same time keep the shopkeepers and other provocators away from them.

Meanwhile the Police Commissioner called Elaben aside and tried to 'reason' with her. He was quite placatory saying that if the vendors left Manekchowk now, he would 'see' later. "You are disobedient," he said.

"Your own President did not want you to do this satyagraha and still you went ahead." Just then some press photographers arrived. The Police Commissioner looked apprehensively at them and made one last attempt. "If you honour me, I will honour you," he told Elaben. "I have no honour," Elaben replied. The Police Commissioner was shocked! How could a respectable woman talk like this! He realised that he could not deal with such people. "You have taken the law into your own hands," he said, "I am leaving; you can deal with any law and order problem that arises." And he went off in his car. The policemen too sat back in their vans and left.

The tension ceased as the police withdrew. The crowds melted away, the shopkeepers dusted off the seats of their pants and went back in their shops. One by one the vendors began fetching vegetables to put in their baskets. Slowly customers began coming into Manekchowk. Some of them, middle class housewives, greeted the vendors saying they had missed them. By afternoon it was business as usual. The SEWA organisers sat in Manekchowk the whole day. Other SEWA members, old-clothes-sellers, chindhi sewers began arriving and sat on the pavement with the vendors.

At the end of the day Laxmiben called a meeting. The vendors were jubilant. Manekchowk rang with cries of "SEWA Zindabad", "Elaben Zindabad", "Gandhi Bapu ki jai" and "Hum sab ek hain" (We are all one).

After the satyagraha, the situation returned to square one. The vendors were back in their place, still "illegal", still being harassed by the police and the Municipality. Could not their position be legalised? Unfortunately, each of the lawyers started off the conversation saying

"Oh those Manekchowk vendors, they really cause a lot of congestion. And they usually cheat the customers." With such an attitude SEWA felt it was unlikely that the lawyers could genuinely represent the vendors' case.

The Supreme Court

The 1981 SEWA was thrown out of TLA. Many women all over the country expressed their support to SEWA. Indira Jaisingh of the Lawyers' Collective too expressed her support and asked if there was any concrete way in which she could help.

Indira had recently filed a case in the Supreme Court asking for a stay order against demolition of the Bombay slums by the Bombay Municipality and SEWA felt she might be more understanding towards them than other lawyers. Elaben wrote to her explaining the Manekchowk vendors' problems. Indira was enthusiastic. She came to Ahmedabad. She visited Manekchowk and had a meeting with the vendors. The vendors were keen to go to the Supreme Court and were willing to pay part of the expenses. Anything to become 'legal'!

In February 1982 Indira Jaisingh on behalf of petitioners SEWA, Laxmiben, Rajiben, Sakriben and Ela Bhatt filed a case in the Supreme Court against the Municipal Commissioner and the Police Commissioner and the State of Gujarat. On February 15th the case was to come up for admission. All the petitioners went to Delhi. Laxmiben decided that on this historic occasion she would spend some money and fulfil one of her life's dreams. She took the plane to Delhi. Since then she is known in the Manekchowk market as Laxmi-of-SEWA-who-flew-by-plane!

The petition claimed that by denying licences to the petitioners, the Municipality was violating their fundamental right to trade. Not only was the petition admitted but the two-judge bench ordered a stay on prosecution by the Municipality and the police. It ordered the Municipal Commissioner to give licences to all SEWA members in Manekchowk area, and for the Municipality, the police and SEWA to work out a compromise solution.

Laxmiben and company returned as heroines to Ahmedabad with the Supreme Court stay order. They had all been very impressed with Indira Jaisingh and the forcefulness with which she argued the case in front of the male judges and lawyers. They felt that with her on their side, they couldn't lose.

But the stay order had put up the backs of the Municipality and the police. The police began a systematic campaign of harassment.

One Friday, Laxmiben came to the SEWA office. The police had arrested three women for encroachment, one of them with a six month old baby. Renaben, a SEWA organiser, went to the police station. In the lock-up all three were sitting miserably huddled against the cold; the baby was crying. The Police Inspector triumphantly said that SEWA could not bail them out before Monday since the courts were closed over the weekend!

These kinds of arrests, summons, fines continued inspite of the stay order from the Supreme Court. Renaben went to see the Police Commissioner and was told that if the vendors encroached on the road, they would certainly be fined, order or no order! What was the use of an order from the Supreme Court if no one was going to obey it?

By this time SEWA had acquired a part-time lawyer who usually fought cases at the Labour Court. He prepared a contempt of court case against the police in the High Court. At the same time, SEWA organisers approached the judges in the traffic court and told them about the Supreme Court stay order. Nevertheless the cases continued. By 1984, when the Supreme Court delivered its final judgement, there were over 2000 cases against Manekchowk vendors pending in the traffic courts.

Meanwhile the Municipality was playing hide and seek with SEWA instead of working on a compromise solution. SEWA sent them a list of Manekchowk vendors and a proposal to solve the problem. SEWA proposed that since Manekchowk was basically a shopping area, it should be completely closed to traffic and be converted into a pedestrian shopping mall.

For a year the Municipality refused to acknowledge SEWA's letter. The Municipal lawyer stalled at every court hearing. He either asked for another date or said that his clients had not received SEWA's list, although Indira kept showing the court the receipt of the letter given by the Municipality itself!

A year later, after a severe rebuke from the court, the Municipality decided to check SEWA's list. It made its own list and declared that most of SEWA's members were bogus! This was inspite of the fact that SEWA's members all had membership slips. After another four months the Municipality accepted SEWA's list of women members. But what about the male vendors? They were associate members of SEWA and

SEWA did not want to make divisions between men and women. Unfortunately the Supreme Court only mentioned women vendors, so SEWA could get its list of male vendors accepted only conditionally.

After this the Municipality delayed convening a meeting with SEWA to discuss the proposal. SEWA wrote eight letters in three months requesting a meeting and produced these in the court. Finally the Municipality convened a meeting with SEWA and the police.

The traffic police rejected outright the idea of a pedestrian mall because they said that there was no way traffic could be diverted. The Municipality offered another spot where vendors could be seated but it was miles away from Manekchowk, outside the main city. SEWA suggested a place be found closer to the main market. After surveying the area, an open plot belonging to Gujarat Government was found suitable. The meeting ended with the Municipality and SEWA agreeing to request the Government to give that place to the vendors.

Both SEWA and the Municipality wrote to the Gujarat Government. A few months later the Government replied that the space had already been given to Ahmedabad Telephones. Elaben met Manager of the telephone company and suggested that the company build its building on pillars leaving the basement open as a shopping plaza. The telephone company rejected this suggestion as too "risky for security purposes." So any possible compromise broke down.

Again the Municipality delayed convening a meeting and this time the Supreme Court rebuked and fined the Municipality lawyer for delay-tactics.

Finally a meeting was convened. The Municipality suggested that the vendors be moved to the top of the pukka vegetable market. The Municipality was ready to build stairs, lifts, provide shelter, light and water. Elaben said she had to consult her members before answering this suggestion.

At first the members were reluctant to consider the suggestion. They felt that customers would not bother to climb to the top of the market. They were also afraid that if they left their present spots, other vendors would take them over and the Municipality would not be able to prevent them. After some discussion however, the vendors agreed to move to the roof if the Municipality agreed to build a broad stair-case up to the roof and if they guaranteed that their old spots would not be occupied. If the old spots were allowed to be occupied, then the first priority would be given to their old occupants. The Municipality agreed to the following conditions:

1. The Municipal Corporation will accommodate members of SEWA on the terrace of the vegetable market.
2. The Municipal Corporation will provide a roof on the terrace.
3. The Municipal Corporation will provide a broad staircase.
4. The Municipal Corporation will provide water and lighting facilities.
5. The Municipal Corporation will issue licences.
6. Until such time as the vegetable vendors are shifted to the terrace and the above mentioned facilities provided, the stay on prosecution by police and Municipality will be in effect.
7. If at any time in the future any vendors are allowed to vend in Manekchowk, the SEWA members will have priority claim to vend.
8. The management of the affairs of the vegetable market will be carried out by a "Topla Bazar Committee" having equal representation of the Municipal Corporation and of vegetable vendors.

As soon as the news reached Ahmedabad, the police department said that now the stay order was lifted they could fine the vendors and began another spate of fining!

As this book goes to print, the vendors are still in their old places, the stay order is still in effect and the Municipality has yet to build the staircase, shelter, etc. The police are still fining the vendors and SEWA's lawyer is still getting the fines invalidated!

THE BEEDI WORKERS' UNION

Organising in Patan

SEWA first started organising beedi workers in Patan, a small town about 90 km from Ahmedabad. Patan, famous for its finely woven cloth has over 500 beedi workers but very little other industry. SEWA came in contact with these beedi workers when Chandbibi, a beedi worker from Patan came to Ahmedabad to find out what SEWA could do for her. She complained that she earned well below the minimum wage and that although there was a medical centre specifically for beedi workers in Patan, the doctor there would not treat her or any other women. She wanted SEWA to form a union.

Anasuya, a young organiser of Padmashali community, was sent to Patan to investigate Chandibibi's complaint. This was Anasuya's first assignment. She was herself a beedi worker, but had managed to study and finish her M.A., the first girl in her community to do so. Chandbibi welcomed her to Patan and took her to the beedi workers' houses. Anasuya found that they were all home-based workers. The beedi trader would give the women workers leaves and tobacco which the women would roll into beedis at home and return them to the traders. They were paid a piece-rate for a thousand beedis earning barely Rs. 4/- in a day for 8 hours labour. In fact their earnings were less than those of the beedi workers in Ahmedabad. This was mainly because they were all Muslim women and so less able to move about freely. All the women also complained that they were not given medicines and medical treatment at the beedi workers' welfare centre.

Anasuya returned to Ahmedabad and reported all this information to the then SEWA president Arvind Buch and General Secretary Ela Bhat (Elaben). It was decided that Anasuya should try to organise Patan's beedi workers into a union and she should also find out about the medical centre for beedi workers. Arvind Buch, who was also President of the Textile Labour Association, said that Anasuya should take the help of the local TLA leader, Prabhudas. So Anasuya returned to Patan and she and Chandbibi went from house to house asking the women to join SEWA and explaining to them the benefits of a union. They then went to Prabhudas to ask him to arrange a meeting with the doctor at the medical centre, but Prabhudas was not home. Whenever Anasuya went to see Prabhudas, his wife would say that he was not home. Later, we found out that he was very friendly with beedi traders and not at all keen to help SEWA's organising efforts.

Since Prabhudas would not help and Anasuya was inexperienced, Renaben, a senior SEWA organiser, accompanied Anasuya and Chandbibi to the Patan medical centre.

They found that the medical centre was attached to a beedi welfare centre, supervised by a welfare administrator, Mr Swaminathan. Mr Swaminathan explained that the Parliament had passed a Beedi and Cigar Workers' Welfare Act in 1977 and that a fund was collected under this Act from a cess on beedis. The fund for Gujarat was administered from the Beedi & Cigar Welfare Commissioner's office, in the neighbouring state of Rajasthan.

Medical facilities, housing grants and scholarships for children of beedi workers were to be given from the fund. However, under the provisions of the Welfare Act, a beedi worker had to have an identity card issued by the employer before he or she could use the facilities of the medical centre. The employers had refused to issue identity cards and so although the medical centre was set up and a doctor was present, the workers could not benefit from it. The medical centre was always vacant and the doctor idle.

Renaben held a meeting of beedi workers in Chandbibi's house and explained to them that they could use the medical centre only if the employers issued identity cards. Chandbibi told the women that they should ask their respective employers for identity cards. "I will go to the Malik" she said boldly, "Who will accompany me?" But the other women were reluctant. "We are only 20 or 30," they said, "How do you know that the other workers will support us?" They were afraid that the employer would harass them or even dismiss them and since beedi work was an important source of income for their families, they would really suffer. For some, beedi work was the only source of income and they were afraid to antagonise the employer as they were totally dependent on him for their livelihood. However most women felt that if the majority of workers were with them, they would feel brave enough to ask the employers for identity cards.

"We will talk to the other workers," decided Raziabibi, a 40-year old worker with nine children. "If they all agree, we can have a large meeting of all the workers and then talk to the employers."

Anasuya with Chandbibi and Raziabibi spent the next two weeks contacting beedi workers all over Patan. Most of the women said that they would join if others did, but were afraid to 'stand out'. But they agreed to come to the meeting.

Over two hundred women attended the meeting which was held in the afternoon under a banyan tree. Most of the women were curious and interested but reluctant to commit themselves. Chandbibi and Raziabibi spoke emotionally about the exploitation by the owners. But most of the women were silent. "Shall we complain to the Labour Department?" asked Renaben. The women agreed that SEWA should complain but most were reluctant to sign their names to the complaint letter, which Renaben and Anasuya drafted. Finally five leaders including Chandbibi and Raziabibi signed and the letter was sent to the Labour Department in Ahmedabad.

On her return to Ahmedabad, Renaben met the Labour Commissioner who said he would look into the problem. But nothing happened. Two weeks later the five women leaders from Patan came to see Renaben to say that if SEWA did not do something quickly, it would lose all credibility. It was decided that they should all go and meet the Labour Minister who had been a labour leader and was known to be sympathetic to beedi workers.

The Labour Minister, Sanat Mehta, said, "you should have come to see me before. I have great sympathy for beedi workers", and he ordered the Labour Commissioner to help the women of Patan. The Labour Commissioner immediately dispatched an officer to Patan who bullied the employers into agreeing for a tripartite meeting with SEWA and the Government.

SEWA was represented by Elaben, Renaben and the five women leaders, the employers by five beedi traders, and the Government by the Labour Officer and the Welfare Officer. When the employers saw the women workers they drew back in shock: "We will not negotiate as equals with our own workers", they said. However, they were persuaded to sit down.

SEWA demanded that the employers issue identity cards. The employers said they had no permanent workers on their rolls. Finally a compromise solution was reached: the Labour Inspectors would look at the employers' books and decide which workers should be issued identity cards. Although the employers agreed to this compromise in the meeting, outside they began a 'reign of terror.'

The workers were told that if they talked to a SEWA representative or to a Labour Inspector, they would be dismissed and blacklisted. When the Labour Officers came to inspect the books, the employers pretended to have lost the keys to their safes. Even Chandbibi and Raziabibi became less vocal and less enthusiastic. "The women are all afraid now", they said, "no one is with us. The employers will never issue identity cards. Can't the Government do it instead?" This was a new idea. Renaben wrote to the Welfare Commissioner explaining the problem and suggesting that the Welfare Office should issue identity cards for the workers. But there was no response.

It seemed pointless to continue in Patan. SEWA seemed to have reached a dead end. "Let us begin organising beedi workers in Ahmedabad," said Anasuya, "Some of them are my relatives, I'm sure they will be more militant." So the organising effort shifted to Ahmedabad.

In Ahmedabad

Unlike the Patan women, the beedi workers in Ahmedabad have a strong tradition of organising. These were mainly Padmashali women immigrants from the southern state of Andhra Pradesh, where their mothers and grandmothers had been active in unions. Many of the older workers still remembered participating in morchas and demonstrations and court cases. These women welcomed Anasuya and said they too had been thinking of joining a union but had not found a suitable one. Godavariben and her 25 year old daughter Kamala were particularly active. Whenever Anasuya came to Rakhial, Kamala would jump up from her beedi work and accompany her to the women's houses. She even organised meetings on her own and insisted that other women join the union. There seemed to be an unquenchable fire burning within her.

The SEWA union underwent a major change in 1981 when it left TLA. Until then the struggle had been sporadic, haphazard and more often than not curbed by the TLA leaders. In 1981 it was decided to make union organising more systematic. Renaben and Neeruben were put in-charge of the organising. A team of fulltime union organisers was built up. These organisers were mainly from working class background and they were chosen for their militancy as well as sympathy with the issues of the poor. The chief organiser was Leelaben, one of SEWA's oldest and most sympathetic organisers who was in close touch with most of SEWA's membership. Kamala, a Padmashali and Sharda, a Koshti were both ex-beedi workers. Rahima and Jaitun used to be readymade garment workers, Mangooben and Mangala were vendors and Indira and Kokila had been contract labourers. Except for Neeruben and Leelaben, the rest of the union team was young, under 32. SEWA was lucky to get the part-time services of a young labour lawyer - Nagji Jiyani. Jiyani was really committed and he had to leave his job in a multi-national company because he tried to organise the workers. Veena who has done her M.A. in social work became the legal organiser. She is now doing her LL.B.

It was decided that the union organisers should concentrate on the trades in which they had personal experience. So Kamala and Sharda began organising beedi workers.

The organising began with a series of meetings designed to find out what the women felt were the main issues and what they felt SEWA could do for them. "We don't know what our rights are", said most of the women. "Why don't you tell us about the laws."Some Padmashali women said they were ready to join a union but they wanted SEWA to contact other women such as Koshtis and Muslims who, they felt, were very timid. Once after such a meeting Renaben returned to the SEWA office to find an officer from the Central Government's Board of Workers' Education waiting for her," We have instructions from the Government to conduct classes for workers in the unorganised sector, especially women. Do you know any groups of such women workers?" He explained that the Board would conduct five-day classes for 50 women who would be taught about labour laws, labour court procedures and the benefits of joining a union; the workers would also be paid a stipend to compensate them for losing their day's work. This was an opportunity for SEWA, the next step in organising and Renaben asked the officers to conduct 3 classes for beedi workers in the Padmashali, Koshti and Muslim areas.

What a wonderful organising tool these classes proved to be! It took the women away from their work, their homes, their problems and allowed them to sit together, to relax and open their minds to new ideas.

It gave them an opportunity to learn about their legal rights, about unions, about legal procedures and about the outside world. It was also a great learning experience for the SEWA organisers. The women openly discussed their feelings of solidarity because for the first time the women were meeting together as workers - not as housewives or members of a community or family members. For the first time they discussed only their work, not their families or relatives or communities and they found they had so much in common! At the end of the five days, the women were usually so motivated that they themselves enthusiastically suggested the next step of action!

Four main issues emerged from the classes. First, no one was getting the legal minimum wage which was Rs. 11/- per thousand beedis. Most workers were getting about Rs. 6/-. Second, no one got any other legal benefits such as bonus or provident fund. Third, the main emerging system of work was the one in which the employers hired contractors to deal with the workers. Since the contractors had no fixed place of work, they would hire and fire the workers as they liked since they took a commission. They also paid the workers less than the employers. Fourth, some workers complained that the employers made them "buy" the raw material and "sell" back the beedis, thereby converting them into "independent traders" and evading the labour laws.

In the last session in each class the women discussed what action should be taken. A group of Koshti women headed by the formidable Bhanuben wanted to file a case against their contractor, Abdul Kalaam "Mister". "We worked with him for 10 years", she said, "and then one day he just closed up shop and moved to another chali because we asked for a higher rate." Jiyani said that although SEWA could not legally force "Mister" to re-open his shop, it could file a case for retrenchment compensation and back wages. "That would come to about Rs. 5000/- per worker", said Jiyani, "I'm sure he would rather re-open his shop." What about minimum wages? "We have to show the employers and Government our strength," said Balamma, a veteran of many struggles. "We have to show them that we are so many and we are not afraid." "Let us have a procession", shouted Kamala. All the women broke into spontaneous and stupendous clapping and the date of the procession was fixed for 2 weeks ahead.

The union's energies were now all directed towards the procession. The entire union team began contacting beedi workers, talking to them to come to the procession. Many of the Muslim workers were reluctant to come as their menfolk wouldn't allow them to go out. So SEWA group organisers tried to persuade the men folk. SEWA group leaders - Godavariben, Bhanuben, Balamma - held meetings in their areas and explained the importance of the morcha. Many of the younger, literate beedi workers prepared posters: "Give us minimum wages", "Give us Bonus", "Give us our legal rights", "Down with the contractors' system", "Down with the sale-purchase system", "Long live SEWA." Neeruben and Renaben planned the route to start from Rakhial where many of the workers lived, to wind past all employers' shops and then to walk to the labour office 8 km away. Neeruben applied for police permission. Renaben informed the Press.

Finally the day came. Neeruben and Renaben reached Rakhial at 10.30 and there was no one there. All the women were still in their houses calmly rolling beedis. "Come on, today is the day of the procession", Renaben said. "Yes, we know, we were just waiting for it to start!" said the women. They brushed the tobacco off their hands and made their way to the starting point. At 11 am about a hundred women had gathered. The organisers were all nervous: would more come? or would we become a laughing stock?" The press photographers had arrived. So had 2 police jeeps - our escorts. But seeing the hundred odd women standing there with placards more and more beedi workers came. "Come on, come on, the procession is starting." Word spread around the colonies and more and more women poured out. By 11.30 am there were over 700 women and the procession started moving by its own momentum, shouting slogan s and cheering each other. As the procession passed through the area, beedi workers left their rolling work and came running to join it. Some came without slippers, many with small babies. One woman was nine months pregnant. Finally there were about 1500 women in the procession.

The first stop was outside the shop of the biggest owner, "Jivaraj beedi". "Down with sale-purchase", shouted the women, "Give us minimum wages." Jivaraj, the owner, hurriedly pulled down his shutter. "Come out and meet us", shouted the women. The other owners got news of the procession before it reached them and by the time SEWA got to their shops, the shutters were already down!

As the procession wound its way down the streets, passers-by stopped to ask what the matter was and the women took the opportunity to eagerly explain the issues. Twice the procession held up traffic to cross the road and received honks of support from the auto-rickshaw drivers.

Finally it reached the Labour Commissioners' office. The police stopped the procession 50 yards away and a delegation of 10 women went ahead to present a memorandum to him. The rest sat down, exhausted but happy and made speeches to one another. The Labour Commissioner promised to force the employers to give minimum wages and everyone went home.

The next day there were pictures in all the papers. A procession of working class women was an unusual event! The effect of the procession and the resulting publicity was gratifying. The Labour Department, which hitherto had taken no notice of the complaints made by SEWA, now conducted raids on all the beedi shops and filed cases against all beedi employers. The employers called the women leaders to their shops, offered them tea and told them, "If you want anything, come to us; there is no need to go to the union." And best of it all was that the rates went up by Re. 1.

Back to Patan

Chandbibi came to SEWA from Patan occasionally just to meet the SEWA organisers. Renaben wrote a few more letters to the Welfare Commissioner, but there was still no response. Then unexpectedly three years after the first letter, the Welfare Commissioner wrote back saying he was coming to Ahmedabad and would like to meet SEWA. He was very cordial when he came and immediately agreed to SEWA's suggestion that the Welfare Office issue identity cards to beedi workers. Renaben was puzzled; what had caused this gratifying response? Later she found out that the money in the Beedi Workers' Welfare Fund had not been spent at all. This had been noticed by some Member of Parliament who had questioned the Central Labour Minister on the floor of the House. The Labour Minister had summoned the Welfare Commissioner and ordered him to spend the money immediately. And the Welfare Commissioner was rushing around the country trying to solve the identity card problem!

Back in Patan the Welfare Officer Swaminathan had been ordered to issue as many identity cards as possible in as brief a time as possible! Swaminathan wrote a desperate letter to SEWA to come and help him. So once again Anasuya was back in Patan going from house to house convincing the women to register their names.

This time the response was more positive. The women felt that SEWA had moved a step forward even if it had taken three years and they were ready to become SEWA members. Swaminathan and SEWA issued 1,500 identity cards in Patan and the medical clinic finally started being used.

Table: **Summary of SEWA actions in the Informal Sector**

Trade	Issue	Direct Action	Legal/Govt. Action	Policy Action
Vendors	Police beating, bribes	1. Morcha 2. Delegation to the police 3. Confrontation with individual policemen 4. Involving consumers	1. Complaints to the Police Commissioner	1. Attempts to legalise vendors 2. Attempts to find fixed places for the vendors
Vendors	Confiscation by the Municipality (no licences), removal from place of vending	1. Morcha 2. Application for licences 3. Demonstrations at the Municipality 4. Satyagraha (sit-in)	1. Complaints to Municipal Commissioner 2. Cases in The Supreme Court for licences	1. Attempts to influence Town Planning of the Municipality 2. Attempt to get Municipality to allot space for vendors 3. Alternative plan for market places 4. Involving the School of Planning
Beedi workers	Minimum wages, bonus, and dismissals	1. Morchas 2. Strikes 3. Confrontations/meetings with employes 4. Demonstrations at the Labour Office 5. Sammelans 6. Negotiation	1. Complaint to Labour Office 2. Over 100 cases in Labour Courts 3. Complaint to the Legal Aid Committee	1. Attempt to include sale-purchase workers in law 2. Attempt to change Labour Department attitude to home workers 3. Studies on socio-legal, and economic condition of women workers

Contd...

Trade	Issue	Direct Action	Legal/Govt. Action	Policy Action
				4. Attempt to include beedi workers under Contract Labour Act 5. Agitation with International trade union Federation (IUF)
Beedi workers	Non-availability of medical aid and welfare funds	Meetings	1. Complaints to Welfare and Labour Commissioners 2. Medical Centre opened in Ahmedabad	ID card to be issued by Government and not by employer
Beedi workers	Respiratory problems	Study by National Institute of Occupational Health		
Garment workers	Minimum wages and other benefits	1. Sammelan 2. Direct negotiation	1. Complaints to Labour Commissioner 2. Agreement with employers through the Labour Office 3. Delegation to Labour Minister	Attempt to include garment workers under Minimum Wages Act Setting up of a tripartite board to handle problems
Garment workers	Commercial rates charged by the electricity company	Letters to the electricity company		

Contd...

Trade	Issue	Direct Action		Legal/Govt. Action		Policy Action
Head loaders	Minimum wages and other benefits	1. 2. 3. 4.	Sammelan Strike call Direct negotiation Agreement	1.	Complaints to Labour Commissioner	Setting up of tripartite board to handle problems
Cotton pod openers	Minimum wages and other benefits	1. 2. 3.	Sammelan Strike call Direct negotiations	1. 2.	Complaints to Labour Commissioner Negotiation through Labour Office	
Papad rollers	Minimum wages and other benefits	1. 2.	Strike Direct negotiations			Attempt to bring them under Contract Labour Act
Contract workers	Minimum wages and other benefits	1. 2. 3.	Strike Direct negotiations Dismissals	1. 2.	Complaints to Labour Commissioner Cases in the Labour Court	
Paper pickers	Work taken away by traders		Satyagraha		Complaints to the Industries Ministry	Paper pickers should get waste paper from the Government offices

Chapter 5

Women's Work and Struggles in the Garment Export Industry — A Case Study of Delhi

V Rukmini Rao
Sahba Husain

E xport oriented industrialisation is promoted by the Government as a 'development' strategy to create more employment opportunities for people. Presently this has become a major source of employment for women. The Sixth Five Year Plan in fact, stresses the need for women to take up employment as a means to improve their status - "The low status of women in large segments of society cannot be raised without opening up of opportunities of independent employment and income for them." However, the effect of employment in export oriented industries in India have not been studied in depth. Available literature on the subject shows that while employment in export industries provides marginal benefits to women, many negative consequences also follow.

Linkage with the world market often leads to fragmented production organisation with passive sub-contracting and creation of small workplaces. As a result, the distinction between the organised and unorganised sectors becomes blurred; the factory exists side by side with the putting-out system which also links the housewife in her home to the world market. Export industries rely in the ultimate analysis on the unresisting, disorganised, atomised labour, all along the line from the free port zone, the metropolis down to the village, and, what is more, on that labour continuing to remain unresisting, disorganised and atomised.

The garment export industry provides a perfect example of the division and sub-division of work and the atomisation of the workforce. In this context, the question of struggle and unionisation assumes specific importance and the disorganised and seasonal nature of the industry poses a constant threat to workers' rights. Yet, instances of consistent struggle to overcome this threat are rather scarce. The industry is so structured that it can easily shift its location, method of production and replace militant labour. While governments in developing countries promote export oriented industries on the rationale that it provides employment, they do not take sufficient measures to safeguard workers' interests. On the other hand, the Governments of several South-East Asian countries are overtly dictatorial and actively prevent workers' organisations. In India, while we have a plethora of labour legislations, the Government does not provide adequate measures to implement them. This renders all legislative measures meaningless. These factors in combination with women's economic and social conditions force them to become passive and develop attitudes which are self-injurious in the long run.

This paper will discuss the nature of the work-force, production organisation, sexual division of labour and working conditions in the industry. All these elements influence womens' ability to organise and struggle for their rights. In this context, the article will also highlight womens' attitudes to unionisation and some of the struggles in which women participated.

Methodology

Sample for the study was based on the economic census data of 1977 provided by the Bureau of Economics and Statistics, and the listing provided by the Garment Exporters' Association of the number of registered exporters in 1981. Due to the large number of closures, samples had to be redrawn several times. In all, 160 companies were contacted of which 30 companies formed our sample. Though some companies were contacted through friends, the sample may be considered representative due to its wide coverage.

From each company approximately 10% of women workers were interviewed. Our attempt was to include women doing different types of work. Women workers in our sample included machine operators, checkers, helpers, thread cutters, button stitchers, packers, supervisors and executives. In total 134 women were interviewed. In addition, in every unit either the owner or a top management representative was interviewed.

Apart from secondary data collection, all information was collected through interviews. Except in one company, interviews were conducted at the workplace. Twentyfour women were interviewed in their homes because one company refused permission to interview them at work.

We felt it was important not to impose the interview situation on women specially after the first few interviews when it became clear that women carried a great burden of responsibility as well as fear. Interviews were closed if there was any reluctance on the part of women to answer our questions. We found that the interviewer-interviewee heirarchy could be broken down by sharing with them our life experiences and information about our working conditions. As such, after every interview we asked respondents if they would like to know anything about us.

One question which followed us everywhere was "Didi hamare liye kya fayda hoga" - what use is all this to us. On our part we explained the role of research in creating awareness and information about the industry. Although we were aware of our limited role as researchers we were conscious that we could learn and get first-hand experience from women workers and their struggles.

Overview of the industry

The Garment Export Industry has seen phenomenal growth since the early seventies. In 1971-72 exports totalled 17.85 crores and doubled every year, so that in five years the percentage increase was 100%. For the year 1981-82 garment exports reached a high of 600 crores.

This surge in garment exports from India is not an isolated example of export success by one developing country. It is a reflection of the relocation of production on an international basis. We believe that the boom in garment exports in India is the outcome of the new international division of labour that is taking place on a global scale and has certain negative consequences for the workforce who are mainly women.

In most South-East Asian countries production is organised in free trade zones. In India, while we do provide free trade zones, production of garments has taken place mostly outside these zones, in urban centres such as Bombay, Delhi, Madras and Calcutta. Moreover, local capital is utilized for the purpose.

Eighty per cent of the exports go to the EEC and the USA. Dependency on foreign markets has meant that the industry faces periodic slumps and while exports have grown dramatically, there is a likelihood of stagnation. We have to keep in mind that India's share in the world market is less than two percent and while world trade is mainly carried out in synthetics, India relies on cotton fabrics, and therefore, expansion of the market is not likely.

The industry in Delhi

The growth of the garment industry in Delhi has been quite phenomenal in the last decade and it has now assumed a place of prominence. Delhi accounts for 60% of total annual exports. Nearly 1600 exporters are registered with the Garment Exporters' Association and if we assume that 25% are active it would mean approximately 400 exporters are active. The Association estimates that there would be ten production units functioning for every registered exporter. This would mean that four thousand units are functioning in and around Delhi. The Association further estimates that 100,000 workers are employed in the industry and 25% of these are women. The latter figure can be assumed to be a gross underestimate because no reliable statistics are available specially about women home-workers. Most of the work in the industry is invisible as official estimates number registered units as only 373 and the workforce is estimated at 13,562.

Our field work has highlighted the following features regarding the industry around Delhi.

i. Exporters are categorized as merchant and manufacturer exporters. The former are buying-houses who usually get orders and thereafter sub-contract all work. Manufacturer exporters on the other hand, maintain production centres. However, they also sub-contract part of their work.

ii. Production is split up into several processes. Each one may be carried out at a different location (except in a few large factories). Exporters regularly sub-contract work and also make use of the putting-out system.

iii. Exporters' units are set up mainly in industrial belts such as Okhla and Narayana. However, fabrication units where work has been sub-contracted may be located in a number of resettlement colonies, in small sheds or homes. For example, Okhla is serviced by fabrication units in nearby Govindpuri. Women home-workers are also found in large numbers in such areas.

iv. The industry has a low capital base and therefore allows entry to many entrepreneurs. At the same time, due to the risky nature of business, closure rates are high. Our estimate for closure rates drawn from a survey of 160 units was 41.25%.

The production process

As mentioned earlier, production in the industry is organised in a hierarchical manner with exporters sub-contracting work to fabricators, embroiders, dyeing units, finishing units, etc. One typical - though there is nothing typical in the industry - production organization is that of an exporter who does part production. Usually the exporters maintain a cutting, sampling and finishing unit. All other work is sub-contracted.

For any production to begin, samples are made and approval of buyers received. The buyers work in close collaboration with manufacturers at the design and sampling stage. Fabrics, patterns, threads, buttons all have to be approved by buyers before production starts. Once approval for samples is received, the following process takes place.

Fabric acquired → Dyed → Cut → Fabricated → Checked → Embroidered → Checked → Washed and Ironed → → Packed → Despatched

Depending on the size of the company and their past experiences various parts of production are sub-contracted. In some companies cutting is always an in-house job while in others the fabricator does it. The level of quality consciousness within a company determines which parts of production are sub-contracted. However, hand embroidery is always put out to women workers.

What is remarkable about this process is the nature of relationship between exporter-fabricator, exporter-embroidery contractor and embroidery contractor-home worker. The dependency relationship is recreated at every stage of production. It is not only restricted to the foreign buyer and exporter. The international division of labour is based on the existing pattern of world development. High technology production is organised in the "centre" while labour intensive production is organised in poorer countries on the periphery. Within the country also similar divisions take place. Urban centres organize production to begin with, but there is a constant search for cheap labour. So that, while companies may be registered in urban centres, production is carried out on the periphery. Main exporters are serviced by fabricators and contractors who live in resettlement colonies tucked away in different parts of the city. The workers who work in these units, in turn come from the hinterland, from rural districts from where poverty and unemployment has driven them out.

The industry employs a number of production methods, the modern assembly line in conjunction with farming out work to smaller fabricators and putting out work to home-workers. It also uses a number of payment systems of monthly wages, daily wages and piece rates. The industry does not follow any one pattern. The only principle which is clear is that of profit; whichever method of organization is profitable, is employed.

Nineteen out of thirty companies in our sample, owned and controlled more than one unit and several of them had control of ten units. This is apart from putting-out work to fabricators. There are several reasons for this type of fragmentation. The important ones are:

i.   To avoid compliance of labour legislation and what is termed labour problems. From discussions with management representatives it became clear that they were concerned about the fact that a large number of workers under one roof could unionise and demand higher wages and better conditions.

ii.   Several companies controlled by the same management were set up to trade with each other and realise larger margins of profit.

iii.   To make maximum use of government facilities such as tax benefits. In fact it was quite easy to close down one company and start another without business or production being affected. The overall result was that while workers were scattered and production was fragmented, capital remained concentrated.

The situation of fabricators and embroidery contractors was determined by the fact that they were passive sub-contractors and secondly, the exporter knew exactly what the production costs were. Every exporter would make a sample and determine precisely the labour, material and overhead costs. An additional percentage was earmarked for the contractor's profit. The contractor was then left to squeeze his super profit by squeezing the price of labour since he had no control over the other elements.

Women Workers in the Industry

The thirty companies in our sample provided direct employment to 3871 persons. Of these, 2228 were men and 1643 were women. As such women formed 42.44% of the workforce. In this section we will briefly describe the nature of the workforce and how factors such as their age, education, marital status and economic conditions affect their attitudes and role in struggles.

The majority of women belong to the age group 20-24 years and those below 19 years form a significant number. The high proportion of young women in our sample reflects what seems to have become a common trend of export industries world over. The ability of young women to cope with high work intensity is often cited as one of the main reasons for their recruitment. Our data shows that wherever large scale assembly production is organised, mainly young women are assigned to do the job. The industry assumes that young women have a lesser share of household responsibilities which makes them more suitable for certain jobs. However, the major reason for employing women appears to be their submissive and docile nature. Young women, likely to be new entrants into the labour market, are more vulnerable and considered more willing workers and amenable to strict control.

Moreover, by recruiting young women, the industry ensures a quick turnover of workers resulting in a continuous supply of a 'fresh' labour force at the lowest price. In fact, in company A, women were employed only on condition that they would resign on marriage. Such blatant discrimination has far-reaching consequences on women's consciousness and reinforces their attitudes of passivity and resignation. Employment in such conditions hinders rather than helps women's development.

At the same time, these conditions made women prisoners of the situation; because of the necessity to earn and support their families, some women were left with the only option - to remain unmarried. In our sample, 48.50 percent women were unmarried and 39.56 percent, married. Two large companies which employed young women on the assembly line account for the higher percentage of unmarried women. Unmarried women are used by the industry to meet its uncertain and erratic demands. Married women with their added responsibility of housework and childcare were not considered suitable for working overtime. But we found that this was not always true and management used this myth for its own purpose.

Education does not seem to play a critical role in women's recruitment into the industry. Illiterate women as well as graduates are employed in the industry. Only four women had ITI training. However, there was no correlation between women's education, skills and the kind of work assigned to them. A majority of women in our study - about 89 percent had some education. But within the competitive labour market, their elementary education inhibits their access to more lucrative occupations. They are therefore restricted to industries whose only requirement is cheap labour and women's willingness to accept low wages. Necessitated by economic compulsions, majority of women are forced to abandon education and accept whatever jobs and wages are available to them.

Economic necessity was the major cause for women's entry into the industry; 63.43 percent women had taken up work due to this reason and 20.89 per cent due to illness or death of earning members in the family. These two reasons are not mutually exclusive and what is important is that women have no choice and are expected to work as and when their family situation demands it. Quite often, men's employment in the family is erratic and this places on women the major responsibility to earn and support the family. Women are sent out to work either when other sources of income are exhausted or when it becomes difficult to manage on existing income.

The average family size in our sample was 5.64 persons. Considering the rising costs of living, large families necessitated a large number of earners to meet the basic requirements of the family. In our sample the average number of earners per family was 2.56 and among them there were more female earners than male. Women's contribution to the family income was crucial. They earned on an average Rs. 313.86 and the average family income was Rs 986.90. Without womens' wages to support the family, 43.44 percent families would live below the poverty line with a per capita income of less than Rs. 75 per month. This is a clear indication of the critical role women's wages play in feeding and clothing the family. While women's employment benefits the family, the criticality of their wages inhibits their ability to organise as it implies the risk of losing a job which they cannot afford.

While many women had come out to work for the first time, others had many years of experience. 49.25 percent women had worked previously of whom 30.59 percent had worked in the garment industry. Their work experience ranged from one to eight years and considering the large number of young women in the sample, it is clear that women took up employment at a very young age. In our sample, for 42.54 percent women, the starting age for employment was below 18 years. Another 21.64 percent had joined between 19-23 years. The young age of women makes it easy for the industry to discipline them and create a familial atmosphere acceptable to them. The harmful effect this has on women's consciousness and status in the industry is evident from their low skilled, low paid work and their lack of resistance to the unjust demands and pressures of industry.

Working Conditions in the Industry

Working conditions in the industry are shaped by the fact that women form a large segment of the workforce and most workplaces are small. Half the companies had less than 50 workers.

Work environment and work intensity varied according to company size and the discretion of individual enterpresent. However, most of the companies provided very few facilities for workers. The larger one usually complied with some statutory benefits (they too violated laws whenever convenient), while some of the smaller ones did not provide even statutory benefits such as paid leave. Table 1 shows the facilities given to workers and the legal provisions complied with by the units. This information was given by managements.

In most workplaces women worked in very cramped conditions. Even in a large factory which had a modern layout the women were crowded together on the assembly line and women checkers sat huddled

around a table or on the floor with piles of clothes in front of them. In
several companies women checkers had to stand and work for the whole
day. Women machine operators doing stitching, folding and automatic
pressing, complained of extreme tiredness and spells of nausea,
headaches and at times fainted. This was specially so in summer. In
one large factory which had a sick room, at least 100 persons reported
sick every day. Common complaints were fever, coughs and colds.
Women also suffered due to menstrual problems, such as cramps. The
sickroom attendant attributed all these symptoms to "pressures of
poverty."

Table I. **Facilities Provided by Companies**

Facility	Number of companies		
	Providing	*Not Providing*	*Not Specified*
Transport	2	27	1
Uniform	3	27	-
	(to some workers only)		
First Aid	2	28	-
Employees' State Insurance	24	3	3
Provident Fund	17	9	4
Paid Leave	11	16	3
Separate Toilet for Women	13	13	4
Canteen	4	24	2
Subsidized Food	2	28	-
Free Tea	6	24	-
Annual Paid Leave	17	11	2
Creche	Nil	30	-

Officially, all the companies worked for eight hours a day and the
official working week consisted of 48 hours. However, in most
companies women worked much longer hours during peak seasons.
Working till 2 o'clock at night was mentioned occasionally and
compulsory overtime for two hours was quite common. In factory A,
women worked for four hours in addition to their eight hour working
day. They also worked a full eight hours on their weekly day off. In
some departments this continued through the year, while in others
overtime work was seasonal. Occasionally, when women worked till

late at night (after 10 p.m.) they were provided company transport to go home.

Though most women considered themselves to be permanent workers, it was clear that the industry does not provide any job security. In factory B, we were told that turnover of employees was about 30 percent annually which meant that there would be practically a new workforce every four years. In the smaller units it was easier to dismiss workers. Notice periods of one day were quite common. Often people were told on pay-day that they were not required any longer. Only in one company were retrenchment benefits being paid. Since there are practically no effective unions in the industry, management had no problems in hiring and firing people at will.

Most women employees maintained that they had good relations with their supervisors. However, others mentioned several problems. In one company supervisors (who were male) took no notice of the complaints made by young women workers, either about working conditions or problems with male workers. In other places supervisors were rude to workers and shouted at them. The working environment appeared to vary according to the size of the workplace. In the smaller workplaces the owner or his wife often had close links with the workers. The atmosphere in these workplaces was more familial and owners were invariably known as "auntiji, uncleji and didi". As a result, women were happy that they had good employers but their actual antagonistic relationship remained hidden. It was in such situations that the need for a trade union was not felt because, "auntiji is so good". What most women did not realize was that they were overworked and paid meagrely. In some cases overtime work for four hours was rewarded not by double time which would cost the company Rs 10.00, but by a cup of tea and a snack which costs Rs. 1.00 and helped maintain a 'homely' atmosphere.

Though women are supposed to be docile, managements always kept a very close watch on them. As a rule, workers were not supposed to talk to each other while working. Another rule by which management controlled workers was to prevent them from going to any other department except their own. This meant that workers who had worked for years did not know what went on in the room next door or "upstairs".

Most women workers said they themselves had not experienced any sexual harassment but knew of others who had problems. In this context we must remember that most women would hesitate to talk about themselves. However, the threat of sexual harassment was very real and many women maintained that they continued to work for low wages only because the atmosphere was "good". The threat of sexual harassment often prevented women from looking for new jobs. It kept them where they were i.e. where wages were low.

In all the workplaces we found that the ideology of the management was to keep women in their place. In numerous ways women were encouraged not to be critical but accepting. If women asked for a break up of their salary (for example, many were puzzled at rates of deductions of ESI) they were told not to bother about it. "Aise hi hota hai" - this is as it should be - was the standard answer.

In all the workplaces, religious sentiments were encouraged. Provisions of place for prayers was made in most work halls and images of gods and goddesses stared down at the workers. The sentiment found its culmination in two companies. In one, the management paid for all the men workers (women had domestic responsibilities) to go on an annual religious pilgrimage. In company B, the beautiful lawns had a well-aired and well - lit temple. At tea time every day a group of women rushed to the temple and sang bhajans. This deprived them of time and energy to discuss issues such as unionisation or poor working conditions. It benefitted owners by promoting among women fatalistic attitudes. It is well known that in several South-East Asian countries, alien cultural values are imposed on women workers such as beauty contests. In contrast we find here a reinforcing of traditional values and ideology through the use of religion. Both the strategies lead to women developing a false consciousness.

The Sexual Division of Labour

The industry not only promotes hierarchies between buyer, exporter, fabricator and home-worker, it also promotes a sexual division of labour between men and women. Jobs in the industry are segregated into those suitable for men and women. What is most important is that this division is not constant but created and recreated to the detriment of women, and higher profits or more control for capital. The elements which constitute this division are:

(i)   Women as a group receive much lower wages than men.
(ii)   Women have less control over the work they do.
(iii)   Women do more routine and monotonous work.

(iv)   Women use skills which can be easily learnt and cannot be used elsewhere.

(v)   Women do home-based work also.

A description of jobs done by men and women in the industry is given below along with the range of salaries. The salaries have a very wide range because of seniority and because in some cases both men and women are doing a particular job. Usually when some women are employed in a category they would receive wages at the lower end of the scale. For example, no male supervisor received Rs. 350 whereas women supervisors did.

If we look at the Table II we find that there are several jobs which both men and women do. But a closer examination reveals the hierarchisation within the system. For example in the category of executives, we find that most of the women are in design/sampling sections or in sales. The sales group we found only in one large company. Though many women entrepreneurs lead production departments they usually have men supervisors. This is supposed to be more useful because men tailors "do not like to take orders from women." In the supervisory category usually women supervisors supervised women. In large factories men supervisors were hired. In some instances where women designers worked with men tailors they always complained of lack of discipline and insubordination.

On the other hand, machine operators were overwhelmingly female. However, here also men were placed in strategic positions on the assembly line where the work was considered to be more skilled such as belt attaching. Though the skill required is objectively not very high, men continued to do some "critical" jobs for which they were paid higher wages by virtue of their skills. Hand embroidery was done exclusively by women and the reason was the greater labour time it required. Everyone in the industry pointed out that women had to be employed because only they would be willing to work for a wage of Rs. 3-4 a day. Men would refuse or rebel at such work. Of course women have traditionally done this work and this was pointed out as another reason for employing them. Checking work was also typed as a female job. Women supposedly had more patience and an eye for detail. What was more true was that these women were also forced to tolerate their drudgery and accept low wages due to pressing financial problems. The same is true of women who did button stitching and thread cutting.

Traditionally, men were employed to do the washing and ironing jobs, industry wide. Usually they worked on piece rates and in peak season and earned a good amount of money. However in company A, women were employed to do ironing when they a semi-automatic drying and ironing plant was introduced. With the new system productivity increased but women workers received lower wages than men. A few mazdoor women were employed as water servers in the large companies. They ran errands and served water to women workers on the assembly line. Very few women were employed in the clerical category and this too mainly in the larger factories.

Table II. **Jobs done by Men and Women**

Category	Men	Women	Earnings p.m. Range in Rs.
Executives	Mostly	Few	700-4000+
Designers	Foreigners	Few	N.A.
Supervisors	Mostly	Some	350-1100
Tailors (sampling)	100%	Nil	450-1100
Tailors (stitching)	100%	Nil	400-900
Complete garment machine operators on assembly line	Some	Mostly	225-475
Cutting masters/cutters	100%	Nil	400-4000
Pattern masters	100%	Nil	500-1200
Machine Embroidery	100%	Nil	450-600
Hand Embroidery	Nil	100%	05-200
Checking	(in emergency only)	100%	250-400
Thread cutting	Nil	100%	225-330
Button stitching (machine)	100%	Nil	225-300
Button stitching (hand)	Nil	100%	10 a day
Washing	100%	Nil	250-1000
Ironing	Mostly	(Few assembly line)	300-1000
Packing	Mostly	Few	300-700
Mazdoor	Mostly	Few	225-400
Clerical staff	Mostly	Few	300-900

To understand the present sexual division of labour in industry one has to examine its development historically. From knowledgeable sources we found that the first tailors in the export industry were women.

The first item of clothes to be exported was the Indian kurta with Hare Krishna slogans on it. Since these garments were exported at a price of Rs. 4-5, labour costs could not be very high. Therefore, work was put out to women who owned their machines. Also the design of the kurta did not require intricate skills. However, once the export market boomed, two things happened: one, orders came in bulk and secondly, new designs and fashions had to be catered to. Women were no longer suitable because home-workers did not or could not work extra long hours to fulfil production targets and neither were their skills adequate to meet the new demands. This led to small workshops being set up which started fabricating on a mass scale. Here men tailors were employed. Now once again women are being employed increasingly as tailors, but no longer are their skills required. Machinery and modern management techniques of organising work on Tayloristic principles has led to women reaching high levels of productivity by doing ½ - 2 minute operations repetitively day in and day out.

While men tailors have control over their work (they are often accused of being 'moody' and walking away from work) and the skills to fabricate a complete garment, women have neither. On the assembly line, speed is predetermined by production targets set by management. As mentioned earlier the only skill women have is to do 1 or 2 minute operations and this skill is totally useless for her to make a living outside the factory gate.

Women and Struggle

Women workers' ability to organise and struggle was influenced by several factors. Important among these were:

1. The fragmented nature of the industry, with its small size and split production. This reduced workers' strength and bargaining power. In case of strikes, it was easy for managements to farm out work to sub-contractors.

2. Mobility of the industry. Companies closed down in case of labour trouble and reopened in a different place with a different name.

3. General climate of repression with the threat of immediate dismissal in case of unionisation. This was complemented

by a paternalistic management style.

4. Non-implementation of labour legislation. Women were aware that owners could flout labour legislation with impunity.

5. Young age of the workforce and the fact that most of them were working due to dire economic necessity and could not afford to lose their jobs.

6. Majority of women did not have time due to the burden of housework.

7. Social stigma attached to women's participation in public actions such as demonstrations and strikes. Families often prevented women from participating in struggles.

8. Segregation of the workforce in the workplace as well as socially. For example women would always eat their lunch separately and unless required by the job, did not talk to men workers.

9. Since the industry is in its infancy, there is generally a low level of unionisation. However, from time to time militant strike actions had taken place but there was no follow-up, no consolidation of gains or analysis of problems. "Natural" leaders were often bought over by companies and betrayed the workers. Such negative experiences led to cynicism and a feeling that nothing could be done.

Of the thirty companies in our sample, twentyfive did not have a union. Three had a union only for men and two companies had unions for women. The latter two unions give a graphic picture of the situation. In one company the union was secret and in the second, the union leader was an appointee of the management.

Table III. Women Workers' Attitude Towards Unions

	percent
Women who felt the need for a trade union	37.31
Women who did not feel the need for a trade union	33.58
Women who had never thought about it	22.39
Not specified	6.72

Inspite of all the problems a sizable proportion of women felt that they needed a union, a reflection of the conditions in the industry.

The women who had an understanding of the role of unions in struggling for workers' rights were very emphatic about the need for a union. As Kamla stated, "A union is a must. With its help we can get permanent jobs, provident fund and other facilities." Neelam pointed out, "I would definitely like to become a member of a union. If we have difficulties we should tell them. Though we give high production we are not getting any recognition."

The reason many other women did not feel the need for a union was the paternalistic management style followed in smaller companies. Often owners were called "auntiji" and "uncleji". Some of the typical answers women gave were "union is necessary only if owners do not listen to us. Here they listen to us. So we do not need a union". "We have family relations with the owner. So there is no need for a union".

The second important reason for women's negative attitude was their realistic assessment of the situation. For many women union spelt disaster due to past experiences. As Amrohi pointed out, "since we work out of dire economic needs, we cannot take the risk of losing the job, which is what could happen if manager decides. Even men are involved in unions only if they have some financial backing." Meena felt that she would not only have problems at work but also at home — "I have too many family tensions already. I do not want to add to them."

Despite all the problems and repressive conditions, the industry has had some militant struggles. Two struggles about which we could gather some information are documented here.

Company B set up a new production unit in 1977 in the periphery of Delhi, with an assembly line system and production capacity of 6000 pieces per day on single shift basis. The company employed 200 men and 400 women at the time and was making profits.

In early 1978, two workers were dismissed. Management claimed that a left wing union attempted to 'enter' the factory. Protest actions were sparked off as a response to the dismissals. Workers made a list of demands. These included higher wages, double overtime rate, bonus payments, tea and lunch breaks, payment of provident fund, provision of creche and demand for equal pay for equal work for women. Workers struck work for one month. The management responded by closing down the factory for one month. The police was called in and a large number of workers were arrested. Though the strike action had been initiated by men, women joined in and took a very active part in the struggle. Thirty percent of the women workers were unionised and of these, 30 women were arrested. Four of them are still involved in legal battles, five years after the incident.

The strike could not be sustained due to the severe repression which followed. Management suspended fifty militant workers immediately and retrenched most workers who participated actively. All the workers on probation who had joined the strike were also thrown out. Management wrote to the families of the girls asking them to return to work. The most desperate workers came back, while many others refused. The workers who came back to work had to sign an undertaking that they would not participate in any union activities ever.

Five years after the incident some of the senior workers still had vivid memories. Half the sweepers in the factory had supported the strike but due to their "majburi" - economic compulsion - had to retract and say they did not support the union. Several women felt that it was difficult to unionise again because there was no unity among the workers and there were many management stooges. The previous union had collapsed because all the active workers were thrown out and now there is a general fear that any move to unionise will lead to immediate dismissals.

At present the workers receive the minimum wage stipulated for the area which is much lower than in Delhi. Most of the workers however come from Delhi. They are now paid provident fund and have fixed lunch and tea breaks. However no creche facility is provided though more than 500 women work in one shift. Whatever benefits workers enjoy at present are not seen by them as an outcome of earlier struggles, but as benefits which management was good enough to grant them.

In another company' workers' struggle led to closure and production was reorganised through sub-contracting. Company C multiplied from a small manufacturing unit into several units in its ten years of existence. It started in 1973 with four tailors and by 1979 there were thirteen units employing 1800 workers most of whom were women. There was a steady growth in business but in 1979, the company's profits plummetted, resulting in the reduction of bonus from 18 to 8 percent. The workers, 900 of whom were members of three different trade unions refused to work until the previous rate of bonus was given to them. Six hundred of the struggling workers were women and their agitation continued for a whole year after which seven units (where the workers were active) were closed down and all the struggling workers retrenched. But before closing down the units, the owner (reportedly) tried to instigate one union against the other in an attempt to break workers'

unity but the women continued to 'gherao' her and put pressure on her.
Interviewed two years after the struggle, the owner was still bitter
about the experience and vowed never to employ women again because
"they are worse than men when it comes to action and militancy". The
ostensible reason for her to recruit such a large number of women was
that she "always wanted to do something for the poor women". But
she regretted having thought that women were timid and peace-loving
and that the interest she took in them had been a waste. She narrated
incidents of how two women agitators shouted filthy abuses at her and
at times refused to leave the factory premises even after midnight.
According to her, though women joined the union much after men did,
they became more active than men during the struggle. Unfortunately,
we were not able to meet any of the women to document their struggle
as it was difficult to trace them. Apart from the owner's hostility, the
after effects of the struggle were evident in the workplace; the production
method had changed from manufacturing at one site to sub-contracting,
the number of workers had reduced dramatically and not a single woman
was employed in the factory.

Apart from the repressive measures taken by employers, women
often have to face constant family pressures and reprisals if they do
not behave according to norms. We met women who were thus forced
to withdraw from struggles or even from their jobs once the struggle
was over. Godavari's situation highlights the nature of such conflicts
and the ambivalence women experience as a result of it. Though she
was able to retaliate when confronted with exploitation at work, she
was defenceless in face of her family's onslaught, forcing her to conform
to traditional norms. What became a major obstacle for her was that
she had a daughter of marriageable age. "My husband was afraid that
no one would marry our daughter if I did not stop doing these things.
I knew that if I worked I would have to struggle. So I gave up my job."

Godavari worked in a small manufacturing unit on a monthly wage
of Rs. 250. She was a first generation worker and her family's economic
deprivation had brought her out to work. She lived with her four children,
husband and father-in-law in a resettlement colony in a one-room
tenement. Her husband ran a petty tea shop in which their son had
recently started assisting him.

Godavari had come to know about the factory from a neighbour
with whom she had gone to meet the owner. She was employed to do
checking work. About ten women worked in the factory. Women did
not have any complaints until their wages were withheld for three

months. Each time they tried to raise the issue with the employer, he calmed them with assurances of payment as soon as the order was cleared. There was no trade union in the factory and taking heed of an acquaintance's suggestion Godavari along with three other women approached an outside union. This is what she had to say, "when we narrated everything, the union men first asked us if we had enough money to fight the case and whether we were prepared to spend enough time. We had to make many trips to the union office and each time they told us that negotiations were still going on. Many months passed; we had spent money and time but nothing came of it. So we went to another union. We felt we were like the blind - if someone takes our hand and leads us, we can move; otherwise we do not know anything. But this union really fought our case. We finally got our two months' back wages. But in our hand we only got one month's wage. The union must have kept the other." How did you get your demands accepted? "In the beginning the union was negotiating but one day we women decided to gherao the owner. We told the union men that while they carried on their negotiations, we would also fight on our own. On the day we went to gherao the owner, all the men in the union stood behind us and refused to come ahead. It was as though we were fighting without them. We felt scared but we decided not to let the car move out of the factory. We encircled it. There was a scuffle in which a woman's leg was fractured but we refused to move. The police was called but we shouted and screamed until the owner agreed to give us our wages. After we won, most of the women and I left the job." Why? "I left because my husband and son asked me not to continue. We have a 'close' neighbourhood. Everyone had started talking about me. Sometimes I used to come home late at night. Everyone knew that we worked with men in the union. And people started talking bad things about us. Although my husband supported me during the struggle, the day I came home and told him that I had got the wages, he asked me to give up my job."

Dhanlaxmi, another woman worker, worked as a checking supervisor in a small factory owned by a foreigner and her (Indian) husband. She was paid Rs. 850 per month. At the time of our interview with her, she had completed four years in the factory. She played a crucial role in the development of the factory as the owner was new to India and depended a great deal on her in the day-to-day functioning of the factory and in dealing with other workers. Dhanlaxmi had a working knowledge of English and many years of experience in other garment factories. The owner spoke highly of Dhanlaxmi's skills and also referred to her "motherly" image several times during a separate interview with her. Dhanlaxmi was happy as she was being paid a high salary and liked the "homely atmosphere that prevailed in the factory". All the tailors called her "Amma."

The factory employed twentyfive workers among whom were five women doing checking and administrative work, and the rest were men tailors, packers, etc. All were paid a monthly salary and whenever required, new workers were taken in on piece rate. The tailors were members of a union; the women were not.

In 1982, the owner decided to return to her native country and production work in the company tapered down. Lack of orders was used as a pretext to dismiss some workers after which the tailor's union threatened to "tear down" the company. All the tailors were promptly paid their dues and retrenched.

Dhanlaxmi who was on sick leave then, was sent for and when she entered the owner's room in the factory to talk to her, she was confined to the room and was forced to resign and sign an undertaking that she had received all her dues (amounting to Rs. 3000). Dhanlaxmi's younger son, who also worked in the same factory, was forcibly kept out of the room and later retrenched. He contacted some of the tailors who urged Dhanlaxmi to take the help of the union but her family members (elder son and his wife) did not allow her saying that it did not suit her age (45 years) to fight. Dhanlaxmi herself felt that more than her age it was the fear that fighting back would block her entry into other factories because the "owners are very powerful and one word from them was enough to discredit me".

Being the sole supporter of her family, she took her son's advice and started looking for other jobs. In the course of our field work we met her son six months after the incident and came to know about the problem. Due to the severe economic hardships that Dhanlaxmi and her family experienced, they were now willing to take some action. We found that the factory was closed down and the owner was due to leave the country in two days. There was no time for legal redress and we decided to draw support from sympathetic friends and a women's organisation to demand her due wages: The following day a group of women, men and children marched to the owner's residence and 'gheraoed' them. After protracted negotiation the owner agreed and paid all Dhanlaxmi's dues.

This action gave Dhanlaxmi a different understanding of the

situation. It negated the stereotype image of the "good" employer and of herself as a "mother" doing them favours. It also gave her some hope in an otherwise hopeless situation.

Dhanlaxmi's case made it clear that small actions can also be effective. However, we feel that this strategy cannot be effective in the long-run. As suggested by a union activist in Delhi, it is important to build area wise, industry wide unions so that workers in each small workplace are able to draw their strength from the larger body.

The problem created by the lack of women union activists could partially be overcome if trade unions and women's organisations worked jointly in meeting the fundamental needs of women workers in the industry.

Chapter 6

Women Workers and Organisers in the Jute Industry in Bengal, 1920 - 1950

SASWATI GHOSH

I

The Industry

T he jute industry was one of the earliest industries in India. It is
concentrated along a 60-km stretch on both sides of the Hooghly
river. Various factors contributed to this concentration: "proximity of
raw materials, availability of required type of labour, harbour facilities,
etc."[1] As a result, in 1929, out of 100 mills, 95 were situated in Bengal
alone. These 100 jute mills employed 347,000 workers and the 295
cotton mills employed 338,000 workers.[2]

Women Workers

The jute mills employed a sizeable number of women workers of whom
90 per cent worked as production workers, "...generally engaged in ...
batching, selecting of jute, sack-sewing, bobbin carrying, roving,
feeding, etc. A few were employed as creche attendants, sweeperesses,
watch and ward, dais, etc."[3] Women were generally employed "in the

batching department as teasers, in the preparing department as feeders and receivers on the breaker and finishing cards, on drawing machines and as roving feeders. They formed a high percentage of hand sewers in the finishing department."[4] Initially the work of men and women was completely segregated. Later, men were recruited to take up many operations formerly performed by women. When the women retired, men filled up those vacancies. Apart from wage differences due to the nature of the work, women earned less for doing the same work. The wage differential ranged from 10 upto 45 per cent[5]

Between 1890 and 1925 women workers increased sharply in number. They increased from 12,000 to 55,000 - and in 1925 constituted 20 percent of the total labour force of the jute industry. The reasons for women's employment in the jute industry, according to Dr. Curjel were: "that women were cheap labour, and steadier than young boys who would be otherwise employed in their stead, also that a certain number of women was necessary about the mills to keep the men content."[6] After 1925 however women's employment in the jute industry began to decline. After the 1940s, employment of men also declined, but women's employment fell far more sharply.

As in most other industries, also in the jute industry women were the last to be hired and the first to be fired. Their number decreased during slumps, (1909-10, 1929-31) and increased when child labour was banned (1923) and during the Second World War (1944-46) when adequate male labour was not available.[7] This fall has been particularly sharp after 1952.

Most of the workers, as well the women workers were non-Bengalis. Especially since the end of the last century, the workers were mostly migrants from Bihar, United Provinces, Madhya Pradesh, Andhra Pradesh and Madras. In the jute industry, migration was on a single-head basis depending on the community rather than the familial migration of mines or tea plantations.[8] As Curjel noted, "the workers from Bihar, the Central Provinces and the United Provinces have women with them and these women work in the mills, but they are not always the wives of the men with whom they live. The Oriya workers do not generally bring women to work with them. The Telugu workers bring women with them, often in addition to their wives, all of whom work in the mills."[9]

Male migration was by and large caused by the necessity to survive in the face of dire poverty arising out of landlessness, indebtedness and declining prosperity of land. But for the single woman to migrate, over and above poverty, desertion, widowhood or barrenness led to her marginalisation in the patriarchal society which would put additional pressure on her to migrate.[10] The witnesses to the Royal Commission on Labour in India (RCLI) bear this out Some women like Gania, were brought into the coolie lines along with their parents and put to work in factories but others like Mungeri or Narsama Kurmi came after they were widowed.[11]

A few Bengali women came along with their husbands from the nearby villages. Other women workers, whether Bengali or non-Bengali, came alone detached from their families and had to "...seek the protection of another man. This protection may consist not only in living with the man, but in working near him in the mill in a position where he can keep an eye on the woman. In return the woman gives over her earnings to the man."[12] Further, "...the average Hindu Bengali woman worker in the jute mills is a degraded woman or prostitute. The ordinary respectable Bengali woman around Calcutta will not undertake factory work. Under the heading of 'degraded woman', I would class Bengali women of good caste and family, who for some reason have offended family tradition and have been cast out."[13]

These women have little relation with their families unlike men workers who "as proved by post office returns, remit considerable sums of money to their homes which are often situated in poverty stricken or famine areas. No records could be found to show that industrial women workers similarly remit money. but usually the man with whom the woman was living benefitted by her wages."[14]

But this opinion that women were taken to be prostitutes if they worked in jute mills, though endorsed by Dr. Curjel and other researchers, leaves certain questions unanswered. None of the five female jute workers giving witness to RCLI seemed to feel this. On the other hand, men spoke of women as 'kepts' but the reference and desciptions showed that these 'kept' enjoyed the status of wives, bearing their children and living as almost equals of their male partners.[15] May be the single women felt the need not only for protection but also for companionship from their male partners. Manikuntala Sen has also observed the independent attitude of women jute workers.[16] The survey conducted in 1952 jointly by the Department of Social Work, University of Calcutta and Indian Statistical Institute, Calcutta did not mention any stigma attached to women working in jute mills, either earlier or later.

On the other hand, Manikuntala Sen writes about a Bengali Brahmin family she met in 1937. Sen noticed that the wife was too embarrassed to admit her Brahminism as they were staying together with lower castes. It is possible that this feeling of being outcaste might have been exaggerated by the higher caste people and the so-called 'bhadralok' (gentlemen) observers and researchers and was not shared by the women themselves!

Working Conditions

Women often worked for 12 hours a day on piece-work. Long working hours and the posture in which they had to do it, resulted in extreme fatigue. Women also experienced vital losses like abortions, miscarriages, stillbirths and neo-natal deaths.[17] Their continuous standing posture at work led to congestion of the lower part of their bodies. This has been forwarded as one of the reasons for their gradual elimination.[18] The facilities women were entitled to, eg., maternity benefits and creches were of very poor quality.

To summarise, for the single woman, her native place did not provide any means of subsistence like land, which the male workers often had. For the woman workers, the process of proletarianisation through induction into wage labour and disinheritance from the means of production was completed earlier. But that did not put her at par with her male co-workers. In the coolie lines, she had to become some male worker's wife or deemed-to-be-wife and do the housework for him. So, for her, gender oppression through the double burden of housework and wage discrimination at work continued along with class oppression as a worker.[19]

Rumblings of struggle

The industrial working class was slowly beginning to organise itself around the beginning of this century. In July 1905, the workers of the East Indian Railway went on strike. This was followed by a sporadic strike in jute mills in August 1906. But before the first jute general strike in 1929, there was a series of strikes in the second decade of this century.

The 1920s was a turning point for the struggle of the industrial working class. The first world war compelled the British to allow the development of heavy industries in India, particularly iron, steel, cotton and jute. This resulted in the expansion of the industrial working class. The facilities or wages of the workers however did not increase despite the rise in prices following the war. This, along with a rising level of nationalist consciousness and spread of socialist ideas following the October Revolution in Russia, gave the working class a new political identity.

The jute mills were no exception. In 1921-22 alone, workers in the jute industry had struck work 79 times. The strikes were sporadic and spontaneous and had little strength to survive beyond a short period.

Women also took active part in these struggles. The jute women were different from other workers, eg., women working in the mines or the tea gardens or the home workers involved in cotton spinning etc. They were different on two counts:

First, many of the jute women workers came from lower caste and class backgrounds and were more militant than caste Hindu women. They had to work as labourers in order to survive. So they did not think that working in the jute mills added something negative to their image. Besides, culturally they were outside the Brahminical standard of womanhood and reacted openly to oppression and injustice.

Secondly, many of the women workers had little connection with their families. For the women, the 'mohalla' or the community in which they lived was more important for their continued existence and well-being. They had very few stakes in terms of social prestige, and hence they participated freely in agitations and struggles.

II

The first women organisers

The jute mills employed a very large proportion of the organised workforce of India. Sporadic strikes broke out since the beginning of this century. As B.V. Karnik has noted, in the jute mills, strikes began as early as 1906. Industries expanded along with the increase in profit in the post-war years. There was however no improvement in the condition of the workers who were at their wits' ends with the rise in prices. Worsening of the economic situation together with the political upheaval of this period induced a series of strikes in the industry. Around this period, in 1917-18 about two lakh people died in the influenza epidemic and many workers out of fear left their workplace and went back to their villages. It was in this situation that workers first dared to demand a raise in wages.[20]

Against this background came the first organisers. Here we shall discuss three women organisers of the jute workers who were active over a span of three decades. The first two came from political and familial background of the nationalist movement and the third was active in the Communist party.

Santosh Kumari Devi

Shrimati Santosh Kumari Devi was influenced by her mother to become active in the nationalist movement. After she completed her schooling in Burma, she came to Calcutta and became involved in the activities of the Swaraj Party under the leadership of Deshbandhu Chittarajan Das.[21]

Though the Indian National Congress did not display much interest in organising the working class, C.R. Das was personally interested in it. Santosh Kumari took interest in working among the workers and making them aware of their rights and negotiating in the interest of workers. Santosh Kumari became involved purely from a sense of concern for the workers and preferred conciliation to struggle. She was one of the foreruners of the organisers in the jute industry and single-handedly established the "Gouripur Shramik Samiti" (Gouripur Workers' Association) in 1920-22 after the successful negotiation in a strike.[22] Apart from Gouripur, she was also involved in organising workers from Budge Budge to Kakinada. She was concerned with raising workers' wages. She raised issues of better work conditions, housing, literacy and benefits for women workers.[23] She was renowned for her personal courage and had whipped away the hoodlums of jute mill employers who attacked her when she was returning home on horseback.[24]

Prabhabati Devi

Prabhabati Devi had completed her M.A. from Columbia University. Her mother Mohini Devi was a famous Congress worker. After her

M.A. degree, Mohini Devi went to Frankfurt to work for her Ph.D. in psychology. At that time she became involved with M.N. Roy and other Indian revolutionaries. She came back in 1927 and became involved in the historical scavengers' strike in 1928. That incident brought her in touch with the jute workers. The workers of Bauria jute mill struck work in July 1928. The strike spread like wildfire and turned into the first ever general strike. Between July 1, 1920 and September 30, 1929, 2,72,000 workers struck work.[25] She also became the President of the Jute Workers' Union. During the strike, workers showed great militancy in Bauria and Chengail jute mills. On June 6, 1926, workers including some women looted the local bazaar, clashed with the police and stoned the European mill assistant.[26]

During the strike, she provided workers with food and paid for other things like printing charges. When the strike was in full swing, the owners offered her to withdraw the strike as they would accept all the demands and provide maternity benefit to women workers. She agreed on her own but this unilateral decision enraged the other organisers as she refused to accept that she had done anything wrong. She asked the workers to withdraw the strike while her other co-organisers (from the Communist party) contradicted her. This led to confusion among workers and ultimately to failure of the strike. This also gradually alienated Prabhabati Devi from her Communist Party comrades with whom she had worked, though she did not share their philosophy.[27]

Both these women organisers came from a nationalist background. They emphasised peaceful settlement of workers' demands through negotiations. In 1946, when Manikuntala Sen came in to organise the women workers of Budge Budge, the workers were already organised. She could concentrate on organising women on their specific demands.

Manikuntala Sen

In her autobiography, Manikuntala Sen has noted that the demands specific to women were: 1) equal wage for equal work; 2) maternity benefits; and 3) creche and children's school.[28] These facilities were non-existent or were of very poor quality.

Manikuntala Sen was primarily interested in campaigning for her Communist Party comrade, Bankim Mukherjee, who was contesting the Budge Budge seat. However, she was able to organise women workers of the jute industry and they came in good numbers to attend the Third Conference of the Mahila Atmaraksha Samiti (Womens' Self-defence Council) in 1947.[29] This organisation was a broad forum of women, initiated by Communist women who became concerned at the plight of the women devastated by the Second World War.

In this period, women from Bauria jute mill showed extreme solidarity with their male co-workers when they protested against the suspension of their leader Bijoy. They cordoned Bijoy off for 11 consecutive days and the Mill authorities were forced to declare a lock-out after those 11 days.[30]

During this period, women workers of Chengail, Bauria, Budge Budge, and Kamarhati, began their struggle for one day leave, bonus and against lay-off. The women from these mills gheraoed the managers. When the unions organised a meeting in Atpur, Mahila Atmaraksha Samiti also joined in.

Thousands of women workers of jute mills gheraoed the legislative council on August 7, 1946. They were protesting against the "Working Hours Amendment Act" which laid many women off in the name of rationalisation. This was the first time that so many women of Budge Budge jute mills came all the way to Calcutta to protest. They defied the large police contingent and finally the then Chief Minister Suhrawardy was forced to hear them out.

In the jute industry, a series of organised protests gradually changed the situation of workers. The first Wage Tribunal was constituted in 1952. The wage structure improved, along with facilities for women workers. However, "despite the militancy showed by women workers, unions remained the preserve of men and middle class women leaders from outside. Despite clear will and ability to fight, women workers failed to throw up their own leaders."[31]

[I am particularly indebted to the articles of Manju Chattopadhaya and Dagmar Engels, and to Ranajit Dasgupta for making available many of the reports cited.]

REFERENCES

1.   Labour Bureau, Report on *Survey of Labour Conditions in Jute Factories in India (1971)*, Labour Bureau, Ministry of Labour, GOI, p. 5.

2.   *Report of the Royal Commission on Labour in India, 1930*, Vol. IX, parts 8-9, p. 302.

3. Indian Jute Mills Association, *Report of the Central Wage Board for Jute Industry,* 1963, compiled and reproduced by the Indian Jute Mills Association, p. 86.
4. I.J.M.A., *Job Description of Operatives in Jute Mills,* Part II, Appendix XVII, para. 10.1, p. 378.
5. Deshpande S.R., *Report on an Enquiry into Conditions of Labour in the Jute Mills Industry in India,* Ministry of Labour, GOI, Delhi, 1946, p.8.
6. Curjel, Dagmar F., *Women's Labour in Bengal Industries, in Bulletin of Indian Industries and Labour,* No. 31, Calcutta, 601, 1923, p.6.
7. *Annual Report on the Administration of Indian Factories Act in Bengal, 1912-46,* Calcutta, Annual returns under the Factories Act, 1952-70, CSO, New Delhi, and Deshpande S.R., *ibid.*
8. Engels Dagmar, *Female Labour Migration in the Organised Industrial Sector in Bengal, 1890-1930,* paper presented at the Linzer Conference, September 1986, mimeo.
9. Engels D, *ibid.;* and Dasgupta Ranjit, *Factory Labour in Eastern India sources of supply, 1855-1946,* IESHR, No. 3, 1975.
10. Curjel D.F., *ibid.,* p.7.
11. Engels D., *ibid.*
12. *RCLI,* Evidence, Vol. 5, Part II, pp.140-176.
13. Curjel D.F., *ibid.,* p.9.
14. Curjel D.F., *ibid.,* p.8.
15. Sen Manikuntala, *Sediner Katha,* Nabapatra Prakashan, Calcutta, 1982, p. 154, (Bengali).
16. Sen Manikuntala, *ibid.,* p.154
17. Rao M.N., and Ganguly H.C., *Women Labour in Jute Industry of Bengal; A Medico-Social Study,* Indian Journal of Social Work, Bombay, Vol. VII(2), 1950, pp185-89.
18. Sengupta Padmini, *Women in the Jute Industry,* Social Welfare, New Delhi, June 1954, p.18.
19. Sen Manikuntala, *ibid.,* pp.153-55.
20. Karnik B.V., *Strikes in India,* pp.58-61.
21. Chattopadhyaya Manju, *Shramiknetri Santosh Kumari,* Monisha, Calcutta, 1984, p. 11 (Bengali).
22. Chattopadhyaya M., *ibid.,* pp. 18-20.
23. Chattopadhyaya M., *ibid.,* p.25, pp.31-32.
24. Chattopadhyaya M., *ibid.,* p.46.
25. Chattopadhyaya M., *Shramik Andolane Mahila Netritwa in Bharat Itihase Nari,* K.P. Bagchi & Co., 1989, pp.93-94.
26. Sarkar Tanika, *Politics and Women in Bengal - Conditions and meaning of Participation,* IESHR, vol.21, No. 1, 1984, p.92.
27. Chakraborty Renu, *Communists in Indian Women's movement,* Monisha, 1980, p. 97.

28. Sen Manikuntala, *ibid.*, p. 153.
29. Chakraborty Renu, *ibid.*, p. 142.
30. Sengupta Padmini, *ibid.*
31. Sarkar Tanika, *ibid.*, p. 94.

Chapter 7

Factory Life: Women Workers in the Bombay Cotton Textile Industry, 1919-1939

RADHA KUMAR

A lmost from their inception, the Bombay cotton textile mills were among the two or three chief industries employing women. In 1895 close to one-fourth of the total lábour force were women.[1] Subsequently this figure oscillated between one-fifth and one-fourth. In 1919 women constituted 20.3 per cent of the labour force. This proportion rose to 22.9 per cent in 1930, but from that year onwards there was a steady decline in their proportion, from 18.9 per cent in 1934 to merely 14.9 percent in 1939.[2] In absolute numbers the peak year for the employment of women in the Bombay textile mills was 1926. Between 1926 and 1939 the average daily employment of women in the mills went down from 35,541 to 21,757, i.e., a reduction of over 11,000 or 34 percent. Since then the decline in women's employment in the Bombay cotton textile mills has been constant, so that in 1975 women constituted a mere 1.9 percent of the labour force.[3]

The Women Workers

The women employed by the cotton textile industry were either married and living with their families in Bombay, or widows who had been forced to leave their villages by the dispossession of their property, pauperisation or ill-treatment by their families. In either case they seem to have had weaker links with their villages than many of the men who had come to Bombay alone in search of a living, leaving their families behind. Unfortunately, figures are not available to prove this hypothesis for all workers, but Kanji Dwarkadas' survey of women workers in the Sassoon group of mills shows that roughly 30 percent of them were married to men working either in the same mill or in the cotton textile industry; slightly over 30 per cent were married to men employed by other enterprises; and almost 40 per cent were widows.[4]

Decline in women's employment

Up until 1930-31 the employment of men and women followed roughly similar trajectories, and the ratio of men to women remained pretty much the same, varying only within a 3 per cent range. The year 1928-29 saw a sharp drop in employment for both men and women; 1930 saw a rise, and after that the two lines diverge dramatically, with a steady rise in men's and a steady fall in women's employment.[5]

The official elucidation of the reasons for women's retrenchment cited four factors:

"The percentage for both women and children employed are smallest since 1920. This may be due to the enforcement of the Maternity Benefit Act as well as due to the fact that male labour can be got very cheaply. Another factor that would affect the ratio of women to men employed is that owing to the provisions of the Factories Act, women cannot be employed at night. The number of mills working night shifts has materially increased..."[6]

Women's response to rationalisation

Interestingly, such official elucidation of the reasons for women's retrenchment did not emphasise the one factor which was treated as a major threat by the workers themselves: mechanisàtion. Winding and reeling, both largely women's occupations, were among the first to be affected by mechanisation.

The cheese winding machine was introduced in the Bombay cotton textile mills in 1925, changing the winding process from one entailing some amount of hand labour to one using machines. In March 1926, women colour winders in the Rachel Sassoon mill went on strike against being made to use cheese winding machines and remained on strike for 5 days. At one point during the strike, the management called the police in to take the strikers off "the mill premises for throwing bobbins around".[7] Inspite of this indication of high spirit, work was resumed unconditionally after 5 days. Mill-owners felt that a strike of this kind was not caused by "serious" grievances but by the desire for a holiday from the daily grind of labour. If this were the case, then this is clear evidence of how women workers resisted the alienation capitalism brought in tow.

Soon after this, more dramatic changes were heralded by the use of the Universal winding machines. The introduction of these machines simplified the winding and reeling processes, compressing them into one. As these machines wound straight into the cheese or the beam, which could be dyed, reeling yarn into hanks for dyeing became unnecessary. Pirn winding too was introduced at the same time, speeding up the winding processes.

Descriptions of the winding process prior to the introduction of these machines shows that it consisted of the following:

1. bending to remove the empty spindle;
2. getting the yarn in the right hand;
3. picking the yarn from the second spindle with the left hand;
4. bringing both hands to stomach level, wrapping the two threads of yarn around the waist and forming a knot;
5. tying the knot; and
6. starting the winding machine with one hand and slowly feeding the yarn into the spindle with the other hand.

The new machines, however, involved only two stages: 1. feeding the full spindles which had to be rewound into the machines; and 2. removing spindles when they were full. This meant that a greater number of the same actions had to be performed in the same amount of time as before, and work became more monotonous. Additionally, the number of spindles under one woman's supervision increased, resulting in a greater physical distance between women at work. Thus the new labour process also entailed a certain degree of loneliness.[8]

The use of these machines was recommended by the Indian Textile Tariff Board of 1927, whose schemes for rationalisation were put into effect almost immediately by the mill-owners. The great general strike of 1928 was against the realisation of these recommendations, and was prefigured by a strike of women winders in the Jacob Sassoon Mill. On the 2nd of January, 1928, 250 women winders of this mill refused to work in protest against the notice posted by the management that from February 1 the rates would be "reduced by 1 to 4 pies for 10 lbs of yarn produced in respect of certain counts of yarn in order to bring them down to standard rates".[9]

On the afternoon of January 2, 350 spinners joined the winders. The next morning all the workers in the mill joined the strike. The management threatened a closure, whereupon the workers went to Apollo, Rachel, G.D. Sassoon and Alexandra mills and brought the workers out. By January 5, workers of the entire Sassoon group of mills were on strike. Commenting on the situation, the Labour Gazette remarked:

> "The dispute was primarily due to the proposed reduction in rates of wages in the winding department but the real cause of its extension to the other mills was the proposed introduction of new systems of work in accordance with the recommendations of the Indian Textile Tariff Board."[10]

This statement implies that wage reductions were in no way linked to the recommendations of the Indian Textile Tariff Board. In the case of the women workers, however, the standardisation of wage rates (recommended by the Board) actually led to a fall in absolute wages.

The wages, however, were not actually standardised over this period; instead, the range of their variation was narrowed, leading to a pauperisation of women workers. The effects of rationalisation were felt most drastically by the women. Reelers were made redundant by developments in industrial technology; the huge fall in the number of women workers which we see in this period was partly caused by the shutting down of reeling departments in some mills. It is unfortunately not possible to give breakdowns of increases or decreases for the departments for the period under discussion since the wage censuses did not always cover the whole industry but gave "representative figures".[11] However, even a cursory reading of these censuses shows that several occupations in which women were employed ceased either to employ women, or ceased to exist as occupations. After 1926 for example, we find no women waste pickers (a task taken over by machines); no women doffers in the Frame Department; no women cheese winders (cheese winding was rationalised out of existence); no women reelers in the Warping Department; and no women washers in the Bleaching Department. After 1934, there were no women employed in the Carding Room, neither as machine tenders, nor lap carriers, nor fly collectors. Nor were there any women hand folders left in the Folding Department: yet another casualty to the machine.[12]

It would be wrong to assume that women were not aware of the potential consequences of rationalisation: the two 1928 strikes are in themselves evidence of their knowledge.

Women's Participation in Struggles

An analysis of what material there is on strikes in this period shows a fairly high frequency of disputes in both individual mills and groups of mills. In a 14-year period from 1923 to 1937, there were 240 strikes, excluding general strikes. Within this, there was naturally a huge variation, with some years revealing greater discontent, and often but not always, culminating in a general strike. Thus, for example, in the six months from August 1923 to January 1924, there were 30 strikes, and by the end of January almost all the mill workers were on strike. The massive and protracted general strike of 1928 was a precursor of 42 strikes, 20 of which occurred in the first three months of 1928 alone. The one-day general strike in 1930, on the other hand, was followed by 18 strikes in five months.[13]

Women were active in about 56 of these strikes, that is, about 23 per cent of them. Interestingly, this parallels their employment in the industry, where they were, up until the early 1930s, between a fifth and a quarter of the labour force. Over one-tenth of the total strikes in this period were conducted by women alone. From figures for "disputes", it would seem that the years of generally increased workers' unrest saw a corresponding increase of militancy among women workers.

Regarding the issues involved in the strikes in which women were active between 1919 and 1940, about which we have some details, over two-thirds were related to wages. There were 25 strikes for increase in wages, either by way of a rise in rates, or for bonus and dear food allowances. It is revealing of the vicissitudes of capital that there were

27 strikes against reduction in pay either through cuts in rates, bonus and dear food allowances, or through fines and deductions, or through a fall in wages due to reductions in working days. Another 14 strikes concerned problems connected with payment of wages, most of which were against delays. The two other issues which appear to have been of importance were victimisation or dismissals, and rationalisation. There were 10 strikes against victimisation or harassment, including two against dismissals of particular supervisors. And there were 16 strikes against changes in the labour process, most of which occurred after the introduction of rationalisation schemes in 1926.[14]

Almost half the strikes in which women were active were winders-only strikes. As detailed records for the period before 1923 are not available, it is difficult to say whether departmental or trade-based strikes had always been a common feature. By 1920, however, newspapers had started reporting weavers' and spinners' strikes, and from 1923 onwards strike breakdowns show that a large number concerned one or the other occupation alone, among which the three most militant groups appear to be weavers, spinners and winders. According to Com. S.A. Dange, who rose to prominence in the 1928-29 general strike, and has since been generally regarded as one of the chief founders of the Indian Trade Union movement, women winders were more militant because they had "more bargaining power".[15] Winding was part of the process of producing cloth, while reeling was part of the process of making yarn: according to Mira Savara, in the 1850s, 80 per cent of women textile workers were winders, while only 20 per cent were reelers.[16] Kanji Dwarkadas' survey in 1941 of the 12 mills owned by the Sassoons shows that around 60 per cent were winders, 16.5 reelers, the rest in other departments, as waste pickers, siders and sweepers.[17] The market for yarn was much less important than that for cloth; in the 1920s it shrunk further, due to the loss of the Chinese market, which led to a curtailment of a number of reeling departments in Bombay in the late 1920s. The issue was important enough to occasion a lengthy discussion in the 1928 Strike Enquiry Committee, especially between Shri N.M. Joshi and Com. Dange on behalf of the unions and one Mr. Stones on behalf of the millowners.[18]

The period of the 1928 strike was the first time that efforts to organise women were made by a trade union. In the earlier strike involving the E.D. Sassoon group of mills in January, both the moderate Bharat Textile Labour Union and the Communist Girni Kamgar Union were involved; when the April general strike started, these two were joined by the Workers' and Peasants' Party and the Bharatiya Mill Workers' Union.

Between late 1930 and 1932, unions intervened in almost all strikes by women, the most active being the Girni Kamgar Union, followed by the Bombay Textile Labour Union. The extent of their activism is best reflected in the Sassoon Alliance Silk Mill strikes of 1932. On August 4, 1932, 84 women winders went on strike demanding a raise of 5 paise per lb of silk. On the August 5, they were joined by 300 weavers (a rare occasion), also demanding a raise in wages. The management responded by giving notice of closure and within two days the strike was over and "work was resumed unconditionally". The next month winders went on strike again, in the same mill. This time their number had increased from 84 to 185. Their purpose was to protest against the reduction in working days, from 24 to 15. The strike lasted for 5 months, with the management closing down the mill and throwing 639 people out of work. S.V. Parulekar of the Bharat Textile Labour Union intervened in the strike and a group of "volunteers" set up a strike fund in September. Little was collected since the workers were by now out of jobs. At the same time, a strike committee was set up with 15 workers on it along with 5 Bharat Textile Labour Union leaders. Through October to December the Committee distributed rations - one payli of rice and one seer of dal - to 550 people. The strike fund ran out towards the end of December. Anticipating this, on October 16, around 50 women workers went to the mill at 11 a.m. and asked for an interview with the manager, who prevaricated, asking them to send a deputation instead. The women, however, refused to move away from the mill gates unless their demand for an interview was granted. At 11.30 a.m., the police were called in to "disperse" them. Dispersed, the women re-collected at some distance and held a meeting in which they "condemned" the management's refusal to see them and the manager's calling in the police.

The level of militancy displayed by women in the textile workers' movement appears to have always been high: in one of the first general strikes documented, in 1914, women were so active that the delegation which was sent by the strikers to negotiate with millowners and agents comprised equal number of men and women.[19] Almost every labour leader who was active in this period has commented on this: "women workers constituted a strong fighting force of the union", said Com. G.V. Chitnis of the Girni Kamgar Union; Com. Sripat Ghone, of the same union, disagreed with the statement that women were active in the union, but agreed that they were extremely militant, "women workers did not take much interest in union work but were always in the forefront of the struggle". Summing up, Com. Paul D'Souza, said, "all said and done, women led the struggles."[20]

Yet relatively few women were unionised at that time. In 1938-39, only 3.3 per cent of trade union members were women; in 1939-40, this figure had gone up to 10.1 per cent; but by 1940-41 was down again to 5.9 per cent.[21] Despite the fact that women trade unionists had appeared by 1928-29, women's "representation" in the trade union movement was minimal. All the three women trade unionists were middle- or upper-middle-class; two of them, Ushatai Dange and Mrs. Nimbkar, were communists and married to communist trade union leaders of the Bombay textile workers' movement. The third, Maniben Kara, was a socialist. Of the three, Ushatai Dange was the most active among women textile workers, both as an organiser and as a representative.

To a large extent, the trade union movement of the period was dominated by middle- and upper-middle-class communists; where male worker-activists emerged as leaders, they tended to be drawn from the more "skilled", even white collar occupations. Even so, it is notable that not a single woman worker was even mentioned as a leader, let alone given a representative position in any textile workers' union. Almost all the trade unionists of the time confessed that they had not attempted to enrol women as union members, despite the presence of Ushatai Dange, though none of them knew why, and all were puzzled by this unaccountable lapse, given the militancy of women. Perhaps Com. Dange came closest to providing an answer when he said, "Well, men don't understand women."[22]

REFERENCES AND NOTES

1.   Savara Mira, *Changing Trends in Women's Employment: A Case Study of the Textile Industry in Bombay*, Ph. D. Thesis, 1981, Deptt. of Sociology, University of Bombay, p. 141.

2.   Computed from figures for average daily employment at the mills given by M.D. Morris, *The Emergence of an Industrial Labour Force in India: A Study of the Bombay Cotton Mills, 1854-1957*, Oxford University Press, Bombay, 1965, p.66 and pp. 217-18.

3.   Savara, *op.cit.*, p. 141.

4. Dwarkadas Kanji, *Forty-five Years with Labour,* Asia Publishing House, Bombay, 1962, p. 98.
5. Morris M.D., *op. cit.,* p. 66 and pp. 217-18.
6. *Annual Factories Report,* 1934, quoted in L.G., August 1935, p. 965.
7. *L.G.,* April 1926, p. 11.
8. Savara Mira, *op.cit.,* p. 155-57.
9. *I.T.B.,* 1927, Vol. I, pp. 204-06.
10. *L.G.,* February 1928. p. 15.
11. The 1926 *Report on Wages and Hours of Labour,* for example, did a survey of 19 representative mills.
12. Information from the 1921 survey *Report on Wages and Hours of Labour;* the 1926 survey *Report on Wages and Hours of Labour;* the 1934 *General Wage Census;* and the 1940, *T.L.E.C.R.*
13. *L.G.,* August 1923-January 1924; January 1927- April 1928; August-December 1930.
14. Compiled from *L.G.,* August 1923-December 1940, and reports in *The Bombay Chronicle* and The Times of India for the years between 1923-1940.
15. Dange Com. S.A., interviewed by the author, December 6, 1983.
16. Savara Mira, *op.cit.,* p.51.
17. Dwarkadas Kanji, *op. cit.,* p.39.
18. *Proceedings of the Bombay Strike Enquiry Committee,* November 14-16, 1938, pp.747-48. in N.M. Joshi Papers. Nehru Memorial Museum and Library. New Delhi.
19. *Bombay Chronicle,* October 15. 1914.
20. All three interviews by the author, December 3-6, 1983.
21. Savara Mira. *op.cit.,* p.176.
22. Dange, interview, *op.cit.*

Chapter 8

Struggles of Women Workers in the Pharmaceutical Industry in Bombay

SUJATA GOTHOSKAR

The early beginnings

With the entry of the multinational corporations into this country in the 1940s, the pharmaceutical industry has been an important employer of women . It has followed the same pattern of creating and reinforcing a gender diviision of labour which has become so familiar in the international manufacturing industry. A very large number of women were employed, almost exclusively in the packing departments; while only men were employed in the other areas of production - manufacture, quality control, maintenance and loading-unloading. Wages were low and there were no unions. When workers attempted to form unions in many companies they were terrorised and often victimised. They had to put up a resolute fight for years till they were ultimately successful.

Women workers had to also face other problems. There were clauses and practices which were blatantly discriminatory against them like the 'marriage clause'. As soon as women workers got married, they were supposed to give in their resignation. The retirement age for women was 55 and for men 60. There was no question of maternity benefits or creches.

"In those days our wages used to be very low and there were no unions", says Treesa of Parke-Davis. "When we tried to form our union, we faced severe problems", says Nima from May and Baker (now Rhone-Poulenc). "The initial steps had to be all hush-hush. We went from one person to another talking about some problem or some general things. Casually we would drop in remarks like - don't you think our working hours are too long?' 'Why should we lose our jobs when we get married, the boys don't...', and so on." "In fact when we first formed our union," says Philomena from Burroughs-Wellcome, "one management person once followed me all the way from work to home... just to frighten me, I suppose." "However there was a lot of excitement and feeling of adventure," says Meera from Parke-Davis. "Some of us were very young... I was 16, but had to tell the management I was 18 as it was illegal to employ anyone below that age. We needed our jobs desperately; why else would we come here leaving our education?...But we had to do something about feeling insecure all the time." This was in the 1950s.

By the mid-1950s to the 1960s, the workers of most of these plants had built their unions, which became extremely strong. The unions were able to negotiate a wage-structure which could somewhat keep up with the rate of inflation, at least to the extent that this is reflected in the Consumer Price Index. In fact, the unionism in the pharmaceutical industry in Bombay exhibited some unusual and distinctive features. An important one was the predominance of independent unions. This is very significant, given the atmosphere of stratification and authoritarianism not only in society at large but also embedded and reproduced in the union movement itself. Secondly, independent unions have a greater capacity to be controlled by the workers themselves and this potential also existed for women workers (then in the majority), to exercise their say in union practice and functioning. Independent unions were preferred by the pharmaceutical company managements from a totally opposite point of view. They wanted "pocket unions". Once it became clear that the independent unions refused to be "pocket unions", they began to retaliate against these unions.

Unionisation-distinctive features

Another important feature of unionism within the pharmaceutical industry was their successful attempt at formation of a federation of unions across plants and companies. This made it possible to take up issues which would otherwise have been almost impossible for unions to take up by themselves.

Some of these were:

1.   The struggle *against the 'marriage clause':* This was one of the most important struggles taken up by women workers and unions in the late 1950s. The woman and the unions began a more systematic fight after forming themselves into a Federation in February 1960. One of the *conditions* for the recruitment of women in the pharmaceutical industry, was that only a fairly small proportion of women employed could be married. So women had to hide their marital status or their services would have been terminated or they would have been forced to resign. The unions and their federation had from 1960 onwards passed resolutions against the 'marriage clause'. In 1964, however, this seething discontent burst out when an employee of. May and Baker announced her marriage, rather than hiding it. On her return, she was served with a termination notice. The union supported her and decided to fight the issue legally. They appealed to the Labour Tribunal. The Labour Commissioner ruled that the 'marriage clause' was being used in order to avoid paying maternity benefits and that the worker be reinstated with back-wages. The management however immediately approached the High Court, where the order was reversed on the grounds that the employment contract between the management and the worker was 'sacrosanct' and could not be violated.

All the unions in the pharmaceutical industry rallied together on this issue and took up a nation-wide campaign. They also approached the Supreme Court. "The atmosphere was almost festive," remembers a woman unionist from Roche. "We used to have demonstrations, slogan-shouting almost every day. Women from all the factories in the pharmaceutical industry had staged a one-day fast on the 20th of February 1965. A huge procession was organised and an effigy was burnt along with the 'marriage clause'. The ashes were thrown into the Arabian Sea. Our mood was such that in some factories, after the one-day fast workers went on a month's strike over other issues."

As a result of their protest, an unofficial Bill to amend the Standing Orders prohibiting employers from dismissing women workers after marriage was discussed in the Maharashtra Assembly. The government put pressure on employers not to implement the 'marriage clause'. Finally, at the same time, in 1967 the Supreme Court ruled that the clause was illegal.

2.   Similarly, in 1977 the unions struggled for *raising the retirement age* of women from 55 to 60 years, as in the case of male workers.

3.   The issue of *Maternity Benefits* closely followed the issue of the 'marriage clause'. The unions in individual plants as well as the All India Chemical and Pharmaceutical Employees' Federation (AICAPEF) took up the question and continuously pressurised managements. In 1961, the diverse statewise Maternity Benefit Acts were replaced by a single All-India Maternity Benefit Act, providing for twelve weeks' maternity leave with full pay, six weeks before and six weeks after delivery. Employers were not prompt in complying with this legislation. In 1974, a delegation of women workers presented the Labour Minister with a memorandum containing thousands of signatures in support of their demand for maternity benefits. Initially, these benefits were applicable to women employees covered by the Employees' State Insurance Scheme (ESIS). In the early 1970s, the unions continued to pressurise managements for the extension of the Maternity Benefit Act to non-ESIS women employees, through negotiations over Charter of Demands as well as through collective pressure and struggles. There were also agitations in individual factories, and by early 1980s almost all the large pharmaceutical companies were paying maternity benefits according to the Act. There were a few exceptions like Boehringer-Knoll, German Remedies and Roche, which gave only two months' fully paid leave, and Boots which gave only half-pay for the three months of maternity leave. Even today maternity benefits can be availed of only by permanent women workers and the temporary and casual women workers, who constitute a significant number, cannot make use of these basic benefits.

4.   The same is true of the *creche facilities* in these plants which were obtained after a struggle. Glaxo was one of the first pharmaceutical factories to get a creche in 1956. Many other companies, despite repeated demands, did not do so until quite recently. In Pfizer, a creche was established only in 1964. In 1983, there were still companies like E. Merck and Indo-Pharma which had not complied with the law.

5.   Amenities like *separate toilets, washing facilities and rest-rooms* for women were also gained by some unions.

6.   Another important right which has been won by women workers is that of *company transport* to and fro, from the plant to the nearest railway station. This reduces the stress and strain of commuting,

especially when the women workers have to bring their children to the company creche.

7. Another important area of activity of pharmaceutical unions over the 1960s and 1970s was that of *struggle, support and solidarity.* These have taken various forms:

a. Struggles against victimisation in individual plants.

b. Support to struggles in individual plants, eg., in 1964, all the workers of all the plants struck work for a day in support of the demands of workers in May and Baker and Roche.

c. Attempts at organising and helping unions in small and medium pharmaceutical plants. Though this was at its peak in the 1970s, even as recently as 1986, there were unions in the small and medium plants whose office-bearers were unionists from AICAPEF. And these small plants almost invariably employ mainly women workers.

d. Helping contract and temporary workers.

Role of women

These were important gains not only for women workers in pharmaceuticals, but for women workers as a whole. Secondly these various attempts touched a wide range of issues and also sections within the workforce. This reflected the interest and involvement of different sections of workers in union activity.

Women were often in the forefront of these struggles. "One of our favourite meeting places was the ladies' room. In our tea-time or lunch-time or while changing into our uniforms, also at other times when an urgent issue was bothering us, we would come together and talk about things that had happened during the day - supervisors' harassment, promotions denied, leave not sanctioned, workload problems as well as our domestic problems", says Kamala from Pfizer. "It is in times of crises and immediate problems that women are more active. You just cannot stop a woman coming to a meeting if an issue in some way related to her is going to be decided. The routine stuff is left to men", says Sushama from Geoffrey Manners. "This is also because men do not have to bother with domestic things and chores at home; but we cannot escape them."

Management strategies

Gradually, the pharmaceutical industry was becoming one of the better-paying industries with a 5-day working week and a wage structure which managed to keep pace with the galloping price index. By the beginning of the 1970s, the Organisation of Pharmaceutical Producers of India (OPPI), the management organisation, was beginning to formulate policies for dealing with unions and strategies for raising productivity. Their first attack was on the wage structure, especially the Dearness Allowance (D.A.) schemes and a policy to impose a ceiling on the D.A. By 1980, there were very few units without a ceiling on D.A. This was a very big blow to the unions. The D.A. ceiling had spread to most other industries.

The managements were also co.sciously planning to minimise tHe gains of the unions and their first target was women workers. Since the late 1960s, most managements in the pharmaceutical industry, with few exceptions stopped recruiting women. In plants like Indo-Pharma and Roche, there has been a drastic decline in the number of women workers to the extent of 12.6% and 47.6% respectively in the period of the last two decades. This is true of he majority of plants. And it is no mere accident that this trend coincides with the abolition of the marriage Clause.

Besides, the managements have also evolved many other strategies to weaken unions, discriminate against women and shirk social responsibility when overt discrimination was no longer easy.

Some of these have been:

1. increasing automation and workloads and *not* employing workers, especially women for coping with increased production;
2. employing contract workers inside premises of factories to do work that was earlier done by permanent workers or should have been done by them as the work is of a perennial nature;
3. giving production out to smaller factories on subcontracting or loan-licensing basis;
4. opening of plants in the more remote areas of the country where labour is cheap and government concessions are lucrative. The company can also at the same time get over its dependency on a single workforce thus reducing the bargaining power of unions.

Impact on women

This trend had extremely serious implications for women workers and their struggles to get a better deal.

1. The number of women employed in the organised sector of the pharmaceutical industry declined. Recruitment of women had slowed down in the mid-1950s itself In Bombay their decline was more glaring in the 1960s and early 1970s. What managements had not been able to do through one method, they succeeded through another.

2. Women's involvement in union matters declined gradually. In reality, they still had to face certain types of discrimination:

    (a) Women are confined to very few jobs and departments like packing and are excluded from others.

    (b) Women's jobs are largely in the low-grade categories. Women who are mainly employed as packers, checkers, labellers, bottle-washers are invariably in the lower-most grades. This also means that on an average women earn less than men.

    (c) Women have to stay longer in the same lower-most grades for most of their working life, because they are seldom promoted as there are very few avenues in the jobs women do. Women get passed over in favour of men. Women do feel very strongly on this issue, much more than on the earlier two issus.

Women in the pharmaceutical industries also felt quite strongly about the decline in their numbers. "Earlier, when there were many girls, the atmosphere in the company was very different; we felt much more secure", says Kamala from Pfizer.

Women formulate demands

In a discussion with women from about 20 plants, women felt that if protective discrimination was one reason for the virtual ban on recruitment of women, unions need to fight for it and its application to all. They suggested the following :

* Creche facilities should not be confined to only the children of women employees, but be available to those of male employees, because both are parents of the children. Such a demand would diffuse some of the discrimination against women.

* Similarly, men should get paid paternity leave of at least 2 weeks to look after the mother and the baby.

* Paternity grant be paid to cover hospitalisation expenses of the delivery.

* Both men and women employees should get at least one week's domestic leave per year to look after sick relatives.

* Also, in view of the tremendous increase in productivity, and to tackle the 'shift-system' argument, there could be a demand for 4 shifts of 6 hours each instead of the present 3 shifts and women could work in 2 shifts from 7.00 a.m. - 1.00 p.m. and 1.00 p.m. - 7.00 p.m.

Dynamics within unions

However, discussions with male workers and unionists on these suggestions were not very fruitful. One wonders why. It was these unions which had, two decades ago, taken up the issue of blatant discrimination against women in employment. Even then it has been a women worker who had initiated the challenge to the Marriage Clause in the Supreme Court but the union had supported her.

One reason may be that unions implicity define a specific terrain of unionism. Issues of recruitment and promotion are not defined clearly as bargaining areas today. In fact, some unions consciously refrain from any participation in these issues. But also and more disturbingly, the unions do share some of the prejudices managements have expressed against women and women workers. From the outset women's position in the job market is different from that of men. The value of women's work is defined by an ideology which circumscribes their role in the family and by male definitions of feminity. The concept of the male as the bread-winner and the women's wage as 'pin money' is deeply embedded in social structures of which the unions too are a part.

Hence, even where women are in the majority, it is the men who tend to dominate in the unions. This has been an age-old phenomenon, right since the inception of unionism itself, and has grown into a vicious circle. Women have been excluded from the technical and the decision-making processes, with the result that they find union work difficult to comprehend and are further driven away from it.

One very concrete case was in Parke-Davis, a multinational pharmaceutical company in Bombay. In this company, in 1972, a woman who was not a union member was being continually harassed by one of her male colleagues, a trade union member. The harassment reached such an extent that she had to lodge a police complaint. The evidence against the man was overwhelming and he was suspended from work. The trade union, without enquiring into the entire incident, took up the man's issue and the entire workforce, including a few hundred women struck work for 28 days. They demanded that the suspension be revoked or that the woman who was harassed also be suspended. Strangely, this is one of the few times that this particular union had called a strike. The workers, including the women, continued to strike till the man was taken back to work.

In the 1970s, almost every plant in the pharmaceutical industry was introducing automation and rationalisation schemes. Newer and faster machines were being brought in. Processes familiar to the workers were being changed and production lines transformed, piece-meal and in phases in different lines within the same plant and in other companies and plants. This made a joint counter-offensive difficult; in fact, on the contrary, it pitted some workers against the others.

This was being done unilaterally, without any consultation with the unions. This process of automation affected women packers the most - in terms of changes in their work, workloads as well as in terms of recruitment of newer women workers.

Women bid for power

The women in Parke-Davis were now gradually taking an interest in the work of the union. This interest grew as new and faster machines were introduced on the packing lines, where mostly women worked. The speed of work had increased and women packers had to cope with enormous increases in workloads. Men were in the leadership of the union. But there were hardly any men in the packing sections. The management refused to allow the union leadership to intervene or to enter departments where there were problems. The women packers were resentful that the male leadership was not doing enough on this issue.

Many of the women, due to lack of experience, were not very confident about their own technical abilities in terms of being able to conduct even the day to day trade union functions. Yet they were determined to see for themselves what they could do in the trade union committee and vis-a-vis the management on issues that affected them so deeply and daily. All the women participated in the elections including those who were on maternity leave. Some were elected on crucial trade union posts. After they took over leadership, they were able to get some important concessions for themselves.

To begin with, they refused to do the **heavy schedule of production** till some important changes in terms of workloads on difficult lines were agreed upon and implemented by the management. Secondly, the women won **time-off** during working hours **for union work**. This is an important demand for most women workers, as women find it more difficult to work for the union after working hours, which are usually fairly long. (This is an important reason why very often women cannot be active in the union for very long, especially when their children are very young.) Another demand the women could **achieve was leave for abortions** or medical termination of pregnancy. the women also felt that the atmosphere between the union and the management had changed for the better. Earlier, office-bearers were not allowed to go to other departments but now the women unionists insisted on having **access to any place in the factory** where there were any problems.

However, when a new charter of demands for the next 3-year agreement with the management had to be submitted, the women found themselves inexperienced. The older male leadership was still too resentful to help them. The women struggled to learn and grasp the technical details of the process. The tensions this process created for the women may be gauged from the fact that within this short period of less than two years, three different sets of women had to try their hand at being the office-bearers of the union. The time was too short for them to learn what the other male unionists had learnt through the years. And once again men could take over the office-bearership of the union.

This entire process unfolded over a period of 2-3 years. Today, the women seem disheartened. Some have also opted for the Voluntary Retirement Schemes and left, but for most of them it has obviously been an educative process. They may have realised that they may need to be twice as good to be equal to men, or that they need a protracted process of collective empowerment of women trade unionists across plants and industries. Today, the women trade unionists are fairly isolated, with no structures available which could enable them to meet each other.

Some conclusions

The story seems to be the same in most sectors of employment. And what it seems to point to is the need for strengthening the isolated attempts of various sections of women workers at self-expression and self-organisation. In a union situation, it is difficult for individual women to assert themselves even where they are in the majority, which itself is not very often. Women workers are sporadically forming their own groups or committees. There have been isolated attempts by women workers in Philips in Pune and in the pharmaceutical industry in Bombay, to come together and relate to each other as women. Men workers have such opportunities nearly every day, and hence may not see the value of it for women. But if issues like discrimination against women in recruitment and promotions, the sexual division of labour in jobs, grades and training have to be seriously addressed, women workers need to come together and realise the relevance of their own experience by sharing information and experiences.

It also seems necessary to form a broad-based women workers organisation, which can initiate, strengthen or support these women's committees and give them a stability as well as contacts, both of which they lack today. These attempts have also been initiated in Western countries, where networks have been formed for textile and electronics women workers with the intention of forming international linkages between workers of the same transnational company or industry. It would be necessary to participate in such networks. However, it is more necessary to form stronger links within the company and industry to make links outside more successful.

This paper is based on research conducted when:

1.   the Union Research Group had worked for the Bulletin of Trade Union Research and Information - 3, in 1983-84. It dealt with the issue of Automation on the packing lines of 20 pharmaceutical

and 2 food-processing factories. Our survey took the following form: 1. We approached unions in the factories employing women and they put us in touch with workers in the Packing and Injectables Departments. 2. The workers we met gave us descriptions of the packing lines, as well as told us about the changes in the past 10-15 years and the problems they faced then and now. 3. Wherever possible we checked these accounts by direct observation of the processes and operations involved and through interviews with supervisors and managers. 4. The information for each factory was then typed out and returned to the union concerned for confirmation and correction. 5. Some of the women who helped us with the survey came together to discuss their work experiences and potential demands. The proposals we made in our bulletin were jointly evolved through these discussions and the whole experience of the enquiry.

2.   the Union Research Group had organised a workshop in December 1985 for unionists in the pharmaceutical industry on inter-union rivalry.

3.   the Workers' Solidarity Centre was working in 1989-90 on a booklet on the extent of job-losses in the organised sector.

4.   the Union Research Group and the Workers' Solidarity Centre were working on the possibility of bringing out a newsletter for women workers/employees in 1990.

My thanks to all the women, trade unionists and friends who have contributed to the information and ideas in this paper.

Chapter 9

Air-Hostesses in Indian Airlines: Issues for Struggle

ROHINI GAVANKAR

W omen workers were recruited in the aviation industry in 1946-47, when Air India began its international routes. The aviation industry was nationalised in 1953. After independence, the aviation industry was necessary not only for the economic growth of the country or for attracting additional foreign exchange; the aviation industry was also considered important for defence purposes. The seven private operators who were not financially sound were brought under the public sector. Two corporations were formed: Indian Airlines for domestic travel and Air India for international travel.

Earlier, the wages of the air-hostesses were on par with those of the officers in Air India. Changes in the aviation industry necessitated new wage levels and working conditions. After merging all the seven airlines, new common salary grades were introduced and the entire staff of Indian Airlines was graded in 1 to 16 grades. All workers irrespective of their jobs and departments were fitted between grades 1 to 9 and officers and managers were placed between grades 10 and 16. In 1953, air-hostesses were graded as category 10-11, which was the grade of officers. Besides, according to the existing service conditions, air-hostesses could work only for 15 years. They could not marry and had to resign if they did. These twin factors - officer grades and the short career - contributed to a situation that the air-hostesses were not initially prone to organise themselves. This in fact seems to be a conscious management strategy.

After nationalisation of the aviation industry, due to increase in the fleet of aircraft, opening of new routes and increases in the speed and capacity of the aircraft, the aviation industry had to recruit air-hostesses in large numbers. Initially, air-hostesses had to complete one flight per day. As the time taken for the flight was fairly long, serving the passengers was less of an arduous task than it is now.

Gradually, the conditions in the aviation industry were changing. Flights became shorter and more frequent and the number of passengers increased. In the 1964 agreement, the Air Corporations' Employees' Union (ACEU) agreed for lower salaries for cabin crew (which included the stewards and air-hostesses) under pressure from the management and the threat of rationalisation. While for the non-technical staff in grade 9 of Indian Airlines the minimum basic was Rs. 435/- and the maximum Rs. 870/-, for the air-hostesses this was Rs. 485/- and Rs. 770/-, respectively. The 1964 agreement was the beginning in the deterioration of working conditions of the cabin crew.

According to Mr. Edaljee, the President of the rebel unrecognised union of the cabin crew, "apart from the deterioration of the service conditions of the cabin crew as a whole, the hostesses are put to greater physical hardship. In the entire routine of serving meals to passengers in an airbus, a hostess has to bend down and stand up about 112 times. She bends another 112 times on her return flight, which means that she performs this unnatural and strenuous operation 224 times in a fairly short time. The strain is enormous. Pushing trollies is another laborious job. Though the trollies have wheels, most of them are not in good working condition. It is very difficult to push in the narrow gangway. It is exhausting work."

Besides this strenuous work, the cabin crew has other functions and responsibilities as per the 1967 agreement:

1. To ensure the maintenance of the highest possible standards of safety and efficiency in the conduct of flight.
2. Maintaining up-to-date manuals, hand books and circulars allotted to them.
3. To be familiar with the handling of the aircraft equipment both for normal and emergency operations.
4. To be familiar with and well prepared for the duties they have to perform on the various types of aircrafts.

5.   To constantly update their knowledge about emergency procedures and be fully familiar with the use of emergency equipment for ditching and forced landing.
6.   To be familiar with agencies supplying catering services on routes.
7.   To be responsible for receipt, safe custody and delivery of diplomatic bags, pouches and high value consignments.

For these functions and responsibilities, the hostesses have to undergo a refresher course every time new types of aircrafts are introduced.

Air-hostesses labour under strenuous conditions for long hours. They have 10 hours off between the landing of the last flight and the take-off of the next flight. The time taken for travelling home at night and for reaching the airport next morning is also counted in these ten hours. Those who stay away from the airport hardly get five to six hours' rest.

Despite these problems, there is no recognised union which exclusively deals with problems of air-hostesses. The Air Corporations' Employees' Union (ACEU) is a general union with membership from all the cadres in Indian Airlines. The cabin crew has organised itself in a seperate union - the Airlines Cabin Crew Association, which is a non-recognised body. Hostesses are members of this Association, but have not been able to participate very actively in the of the union activities. Apart from the problems most working women face, the specific handicaps of air-hostesses are as follows:

1.   Their working hours and work schedules are such that they hardly ever meet each other to discuss common issues. The only time they meet in at least a small group is when they have stand-by duties.
2.   Unlike their male colleagues, the stewards, they have family responsibilities. This is especially true of married hostesses. Often husbands and in-laws are not very cooperative and many hostesses are on the defensive due to their odd working hours and often compensate by working harder at home too.

Problems air-hostesses face at work include:

1. There are no promotional avenues for hostesses. There is only one post of Chief Air-hostess for each base and one post of Deputy Chief Air-hostess (Indian Airlines has only 4 bases in India).

2. The normal flight-time is from 6 a.m. to 10 p.m. If the flight is delayed, according to the 1972 agreement, hostesses were entitled to a 24 hours rest period; the 1982 agreement reduced this to 12 hours. Hostesses have indefinite hours of duty when flights are delayed. They are not paid any overtime in such cases.

3. According to the 1982 circular of the Director of Operations, if a couple worked on board , they were to be given common flights. After 1985 however, this circular has been ignored and the two partners are sent on different flights.

4. Working hours are calculated on the basis of "engine on and engine off". If there is any delay or disturbance before "engine on" or after "engine off", this delayed time is not calculated in the flying hours.

The special grievances of air-hostesses are:

1. Pursers could get married immediately after recruitment or even married men were taken as flight pursers. Hostesses however had to wait for four years after recruitment before they could marry. After a prolonged struggle, this clause was struck down in 1989.

2. A purser may have any number of children,; the hostess may not have more than two living children.

3. Earlier, the superannuation age for hostesses was thirty-five years after which they had to go for a full medical check-up every year and obtain a fitness certificate each year; only then could they continue to work upto 58 years. The superannuation for men is 55 years and they can continue upto 58 years without any medical check-up. After years of struggle and court battles, the age of superannuation for hostesses has been extended to 58 years only recently in October 1989.

4. Hostesses have to go on leave as soon as pregnancy is confirmed. They have to use all their sick leave, casual leave and whatever privilege leave is to their credit. They are

legally entitled to maternity leave for only 48 days before and 42 days after delivery. They have to invariably take many months off both before and after delivery.

Despite these serious issues, during the last 35 years, there have been no women on the executive of the union or even as committee members. This is true of both the hostesses and women workers of the commercial and administrative aviation staff. Women have not been able to play a role at the decision-making levels of the union. However, the picture seems to be changing over the last few years. Circumstances are forcing hostesses to unite and become vocal.

One such struggle waged by the hostesses was when one woman, Ms Kadri was taken off the roster for an alleged misbehaviour during the flight. Management could have framed charges against her and suspended her pending enquiry. However, the entire crew went into action and the problem was resolved after a strike of three hours.

The hostesses have fought a series of legal battles too. They were able to raise the age of retirement through a consistent and determined struggle at the Supreme Court level. This struggle and the decision itself will bring about a change in the attitude of hostesses as now with the increase in the age of retirement, the hostesses have a greater stake in their work and career.

Chapter 10

Women Teachers in the Delhi University Teachers' Strike

Shaswati Mazumdar

T he 74-day long Delhi University teachers' strike which ended on 22nd February 1986 roused feelings of both indignation and inspiration in different sections of the people. The large scale participation by women teachers was demonstrative and visible and found expression in photographs and reports in the press. For those of us who were involved in this physically and mentally exhausting but also exhilarating strike, the large scale participation by women teachers was one of the most significant measures of the success of the strike and of the striking power of the Delhi University Teachers' Association (DUTA).

Factors influencing women teachers' attitudes to struggles

Although many women teach in co-educational colleges, a large number of women are concentrated in the 15 women's colleges. These colleges are not all the same - some are very old colleges with a relatively large contingent of senior teachers, others are newer with predominantly younger teachers. Problems and experiences differ and so do traditions of participation in struggles; some are so-called minority colleges, some are professional colleges, some are run by private trusts, some come under the Delhi Administration, some are maintained directly by the University. Nevertheless, certain characteristic features can be identified which are linked to the all-women (or predominantly women) membership of the teaching staff.

In our society with its hierarchical social structure and ideological moorings, women teachers like women in other professions still carry the double burden of professional work and family and household responsibilities. These extra responsibilities physically interfere with and inhibit active participation. Moreover, the social morality which supports and reinforces this role makes women the butt of authoritarian decision-making. At the same time, it ideologically inhibits association with trade unionism and political movements. The resulting lack of awareness and information further reinforces the social role imposed on them and makes them far more vulnerable than their men collegues.

Governing bodies of colleges are also generally undemocratic, and do not have even a single elected teacher representative. However, governing bodies of women's colleges are characterised by greater authoritarianism in their dealings with teachers. A number of incidents during the strike exemplified this.

Another factor which influences women's attitudes is that many of them are first generation job-holders in a society in which unemployment is perhaps more rampant amongst educated women than amongst educated men. This lends a certain sense of insecurity to women teachers when confronted with repressive measures threatening security of service, which is further compounded by lack of agitational experience.

The role of the family and more specifically of the husbands cannot also be overlooked. Where the husbands are also Delhi University teachers, interests are commonly perceived. But many women are married to members of the bureaucracy and of other professions. The professional interests of such women as second income earners also become secondary. Pressure from the family, especially from the husband also inhibits participation.

Their participation in actions on different issues showed that women teachers respond less to mobilisation on purely economic issues. Many of them do not see their primary role as bread earners. It was our experience that women teachers are far more active on issues of democratic rights, educational policy, etc. At the time of the 1982-83 strike, their participation in the fight against the Hospitals and Other Institutions' Bill (aimed at restricting teachers' democratic rights) contributed greatly in making this a focal point in the initial stages of the strike when this Bill was being debated in Parliament. Similarly, in the last strike and after its withdrawal, the interest generated in the New Education Policy was far greater in the women's colleges. Most of the meetings and seminars organised on this Policy were held in women's colleges and women teachers were vocal in opposing its elitist, anti-democratic character.

An ideological weapon used by the authorities against the entire teaching community but with somewhat greater success against the women teachers is the constant reminder of their commitment to their students. It is almost considered sinful for teachers to strike work. The social morality which defines women's role in our society also makes them easy victims of this ideological stick. However, it is important that commitment to students has been deliberately interpreted in the narrow sense of taking classes, completing courses, ensuring that examinations are held and results declared on time. The ruling classes have never sought fit to even encourage the social role of teachers in questioning the evils of our society, suggesting remedies, participating in movements for social change and developing in the students a scientific and democratic bent of mind. The special responsibility of women teachers towards their girl students has, of course been utterly neglected. Girl students often look up to their women teachers for models of social behaviour. This is especially true about those who are first generation students or in whose families no women are working outside the house. Despite the physical and ideological hindrances outlined above and sometimes in direct confrontation with them, women teachers participated in the 1982-83 strike and in the 1985-86 strike visibly, actively and with growing determination. The process of radicalisation in many of them was quite remarkable, at times surprising not only the general public but even activists of DUTA who had a cynical attitude on women's participation.

DUTA and women's participation since the Emergency

In the 40 years since Independence, the teaching community like other sections of the working people has experienced an erosion of its economic and other rights. Educational policy, which should have aimed at smashing the colonial ideological hold by wiping out illiteracy, universalising primary education and expanding and developing higher education, deliberately did not take on this task with the necessary determination. Instead it grew steadily more elitist excluding the majority of the people of this country from the purview of any kind of education. Coupled with this were increasing attacks on the democratic rights of students and teachers, University autonomy and academic freedom. Government's attitude towards the restless teaching community was increasing authoritarianism. This came to a head during the Emergency with the suppression of all democratic rights through terror, large scale arrests and the disfunctionalisation of teachers' associations. With the defeat of the party which had ruled this country since Independence and imposed the emergency, a new life surged into mass movements of all sections of the people and also into the teachers' associations. This is the background against which the history of DUTA and the role of its women members has to be viewed.

An explanatory note on DUTA's political composition becomes essential. Broadly, three political forces are represented in DUTA. Two of these are the two major political forces which dominate Delhi city politics, the Congress (I) and the Bharatiya Janata Party (BJP). The third political force is that of the left and democratic sections mainly represented in the Delhi University based teachers' organisation, the Democratic Teachers' Front.

The election procedure is such that each of these three political forces find representation in DUTA's Executive Committee. Only the President is directly elected. Other office-bearers are elected by the Executive Committee.

While the president by virtue of being directly elected enjoys a certain initiative, democratic decision-making - a prerequisite for united struggle - demands support to this initiative from the Executive and support to the Executive from the General Body. A leadership committed to the politics of united struggle derives its ultimate strength from a mobilised and active General Body. Since around 40% of the teachers in the Delhi University and its colleges are women, the implications of such a politics are clear.

Immediately after the lifting of Emergency, DUTA was in a state of shock, disorganisation and apathy and not yet in a position to organise on a large scale for long-pending demands. General Body meetings were poorly attended; token actions were unable to create any impression on the authorities due to low participation. The absence of women teachers in both meetings and actions was marked.

Besides the factors inhibiting women's participation already mentioned earlier, certain factors internal to DUTA were also responsible for this weakness. The atmosphere dominating DUTA activities, whether meetings or token actions, in the period just preceding the Emergency and even for a while after March 1977, was not conducive to women's participation. Vested interest groups not inclined to watch DUTA develop a perspective of united struggle provoked incidents of physical violence and verbal indecency which dissuaded women teachers from participating. DUTA members, men and women, were more conscious of disunity on political and other lines than of their unity as a professional group with common problems and demands. In fact, DUTA leadership during this period showed scant respect for the General Body, often not allowing it to meet on flimsy grounds. Similar tactics were employed even with requisitioned meetings. The traumatic experience of the Emergency and the long period of inactivity resulted in apathy and a feeling of impotence which was more marked in the case of women teachers. These factors contributed in keeping the politics of united struggle at bay.

However, after the Emergency and specifically since 1979-80, DUTA slowly, haltingly but surely moved to adopt a perspective of united struggle. A Charter of Demands was adopted.

An interesting incident characteristic of that stage in the history of DUTA is associated with the adoption of this Charter. A suggestion had been mooted by some members at a meeting of DUTA Executive to include the demand for creche facilities in the Charter. Not receiving an encouraging response from the Executive, these members decided to take up the issue with the women teachers. A signature campaign was conducted and the signatures were placed before the General Body which was meeting to adopt the Charter. In full public view some members associated with a conservative political group chose to jeer at this demand. Nevertheless, the General Body voted to include creche facilities in the Charter.

The major demands in the Charter were for a non-arbitrary, non-quota based promotion scheme which would give every teacher atleast one promotion in a lifetime, housing (which was eating up atleast half of teachers' salaries) and some economic relief for teachers stagnating at the top of the selection grade.

The period from 1979-81 saw many mass scale actions by DUTA for the realisation of this Charter. On occasions more than 1500 teachers participated in actions; of these, 40% were women. Gradually, the capacity of DUTA for intervention was also increasing, finally forcing the Executive Council of the University to set up a committee on our Charter which submitted a report known as the Mathur Committee report. The Mathur Committee took a favourable view on many of our demands.

It is necessary to mention here an incident which once again sharply brought into focus the pressure on DUTA to respond to women's demands. A woman teacher from one of the women's colleges committed suicide. Colleagues from her college, distressed and dissatisfied with the indifferent attitude of the police, conducted their own investigations and discovered that prior to the death, demands for relatively large sums of money had been made on her and through her on her parents. All the more shocking was the fact that her husband was also a teacher in another Delhi University college.

Having failed to elicit any response for a thorough investigation from all levels of the police hierarchy, the teachers of this women's college came en masse to DUTA for help. Under pressure from the teachers who were supported by the progressive and democratic sections within the DUTA leadership, the DUTA Executive decided to set up a DUTA enquiry committee to investigate the circumstances leading to the death. This decision was especially controversial as the husband of the woman who had died was also a member of DUTA, and had the support of a conservative political group amongst the teachers. More significant however, was that some of the concerned women teachers raised the issue despite their links with the same political group.

The DUTA enquiry committee submitted a report after completing investigations which alleged involvement by the husband and in-laws in the circumstances leading to the death. A copy of this report was submitted to the Commissioner of Police. However, as was the case in almost all dowry death incidents at that time, inadequate evidence under existing laws and lack of a will to implement even these laws led to the dropping of such cases or their fading into oblivion; in this case too, the matter could not be pursued. Though in terms of bringing the guilty to book no success was achieved, yet this incident contributed to raising the consciousness of both, the concerned women teachers and of DUTA. These women teachers themselves realised and then made the DUTA realise that this was an issue which an association committed to protect the interests of its members had to take up. At the same time they realised the need for active intervention on their own part. This was vividly demonstrated in the increasing participation of the women teachers in the anti-dowry demonstrations organised by almost all women's organisations under the banner of the Dahej Virodhi Chetna Manch. The incident was a landmark in the history of DUTA setting certain norms and standards of behaviour for its members.

Lack of will on the part of the authorities to implement even the recommendations of the Mathur Committee and the continuing indifference to the increasing hardships of the teachers compelled the latter, and therefore DUTA, to seriously consider an indefinite strike. On 8th October 1982 the General Body adopted the recommendation of the DUTA Executive to proceed on strike from 12th October.

The teachers continued to strike work for 109 days, thus creating history. This was the longest teachers' strike in this country. The General Body met more than 7 times, each time voting to continue the strike in view of the unchanging indifference of the authorities to their demands. Women teachers thronged the meetings occupying the front benches, sometimes even bringing their children with them. Participation in these meetings went up to 2,000 or more. While men teachers in general came to General Body meetings individually or at best with friends, teachers representing women's colleges tended to come together. Often they took the college bus or hired a private bus for the purpose. It was also common for the women's college staff associations to meet prior to the General Body meetings and elect a delegation to represent them at the meeting. Women teachers were also persistent in suggesting more participative actions and abhorred the idea of having to sit most of the days at home. They did not want to treat the strike as a holiday.

After more than a 2 month long period of indifference by the authorities, the refusal of the teachers to be disheartened or cowed down began to draw public attention. The Government reluctantly started negotiations in early January 1983, but remained unwilling to come to an amicable settlement. Meanwhile, the parent of a Delhi University student filed a case in the High Court against DUTA. In fact, this widely publicised case exposed to the public eye the genuineness of teachers' grievances and the legitimacy of their demands. The continuing strike, the revelations in the High Court hearings, the growing sympathy in the press and the political pressure of the impending Delhi Metropolitan elections forced the Government to the negotiating table. From these negotiations emerged an agreement on the basis of which the DUTA General Body called off the strike on 29th January 1983.

The January 1983 Agreement conceded an ongoing promotion

scheme based on seniority and without any quota (subsequently incorporated into the Ordinances of the University); funds for housing, and acceptance in principle of the demands for relief to stagnating selection grade teachers and introduction of professors' grade in colleges.

The 1985-86 Strike

Almost two years later, the DUTA General Body at its meeting held on 15th December 1985 noted that the authorities had betrayed the 1983 Agreement. The promotion scheme had been unilaterally withdrawn by the UGC despite the fact that it was now part of the University Ordinances; most other parts of the Agreement remained unimplemented. The General Body further noted that the authorities had failed to respond to any number of letters, representations, dharnas, demonstrations and even a one-day strike action. The General Body therefore, unanimously approved the recommendation of the DUTA Executive to proceed on strike from 10th December 1985.

Unlike at the time of the previous strike, the Government was not entirely indifferent to the strike threat and showed preparedness to negotiate even a week before the actual commencement of the strike. Perhaps an agreement could have been arrived at and the strike averted if it had not been for the Government's determination to introduce the New Education Policy including drastic changes in University structure and governance and teachers' service conditions. It must be admitted that this was not obvious to us at that time. Subsequent developments during the course of the strike and thereafter has sharply brought into focus the contradiction between the 1983 Agreement and Government's plans in the field of higher education.

During the first three weeks of December several meetings took place with the Government, the UGC and University representatives. As an office-bearer of DUTA , I was physically present at all these meetings. An interesting feature of the method of argument of Government representatives was the belief that DUTA office-bearers could convince the General Body to accept half-hearted concessions. This stemmed from the false premise that DUTA was a pocket organisation of its leaders, a set of trouble-makers who had provoked the strike and who could call it off merely on the basis of rhetoric and argumentative ability. Government intelligence was inefficient in reporting the high level of information in the mass of DUTA members with regard to the issues of the strike.

It is in this well-informed membership that the strength of DUTA lay. Detailed newsletters and reporting in General Body meetings, regular visits by DUTA activists to meetings of college staff associations was standard practice. On one occasion, even a house to house information campaign was launched. The Delhi University and its 56 colleges are spread over the entire length and breadth of Delhi. The difficulty of the task of keeping the more than 5,000 members of DUTA informed can therefore, well be imagined. However, the basis for united struggle was an informed membership and those committed to this struggle did not spare themselves in tackling this difficult but rewarding task.

As pointed out earlier, teachers in women's colleges for various reasons tend to be less aware, less well-informed. The DUTA leadership, aware of this problem, consciously adopted strategies to break this information barrier. As a result, women's colleges were amongst those most frequently visited by DUTA activists. The mobilisation of women teachers was time-consuming. Yet it is also a fact that once convinced of the correctness of the path adopted, women teachers went through a remarkable process of radicalisation, discarding age-old prejudices and looking at their role anew. This in turn had a tremendous morale-boosting effect both on individual DUTA activists and on the DUTA Executive.

It was more than a month after the strike began that the authorities agreed to honour their commitments made in 1983 with regard to the ongoing promotion scheme, housing and relief to stagnating selection grade teachers. However, they remained adamant in refusing to honour that grade in college. On 22nd January 1986, the DUTA General Body therefore, resolved to continue the strike.

Several tactics were used to counter and break the strike--outright denial that the introduction of professor's grade in colleges had formed part of the 1983 Agreement, attempts to divide the teachers in University departments and in colleges, in men's colleges and in women's colleges, a vilification campaign in the media, particularly on Doordarshan, and last, but not least, unprecedented repressive measures.

The DUTA withstood all these moves and considerable credit for this goes to its women members. On 30th January, under instruction from the UGC and bypassing the University Executive Council, the college managements implemented the non-payment of the January salaries to striking teachers. The Vice-Chancellor chose neither to challenge this blatant attack on University autonomy by the UGC nor to implement the UGC notification in the case of the University department teachers. The latter was clearly aimed at creating a rift between the University department and college teachers.

Three days later the Vice-Chancellor went a step further, issuing a notification threatening the service conditions of teachers who did not report back to work by 6th February. The wording of the notification was deliberately vague in order to create the maximum confusion and generate fear.

Such repressive measures are a common experience in working class struggles. But never before in the history of DUTA have teachers experienced a wage cut or a threat to their service conditions. Yet they reacted valiantly to rebuff these attempts to break their unity. Solidarity with and loyalty to DUTA became the pass-word. Especially the women teachers were affronted and indignant at the direct attack on their democratic rights, their dignity and self-respect. They demonstrated their anger by participating in the 3-day court arrest action (4th, 5th and 6th February 1986) in ever larger numbers, surprising the Delhi public, the DUTA leadership and particularly, I think, even themselves. For most of them this was the first time they had participated in such an action.

Following the repressive measures, governing bodies, especially of women's colleges, tried to take advantage of the situation to threaten, terrorise and browbeat teachers, individually and in groups.

In Mata Sundri College the Chairman of the governing body issued letters threatening outright dismissal if teachers did not return to work on a specified date. Confusion and fear prevailed for some time egged on by anti-strike elements within DUTA. Nevertheless, the staff association of the college met on the day they were to return to work and displayed great courage by unanimously resolving to stay with the strike. In Vivekanand Mahila College, the Chairman of the governing body intruded into a staff association meeting and threatened teachers with all manner of consequences. The day before, he along with other members of the educational bureaucracy had appealed to the Prime Minister, both through the newspapers and on Doordarshan, to declare the strike illegal and to bring it under the purview of the Essential Services Maintenance Act. Many teachers were unnerved. But again they overcame these fears and continued their support to DUTA.

The Chairman of another women's college tried another tactic. He told a group of teachers who had gone to submit a memorandum protesting against the wage cut that the DUTA was in the hands of a bunch of communists who wanted to create countrywide disturbances aimed at disrupting the unity and integrity of the country. The above incidents are indicative of the many and varied tactics employed by college managements to force their teaching staff to break the strike.

However, even after the court arrest action, a high level of participation was maintained right through the subsequent days of the strike. This culminated in the march to Parliament on 21st February 1986 in which over 2,500 teachers, of whom at least a thousand were women, walked along a 6 kilometre route to submit a memorandum on the betrayal of the 1983 Agreement. On the next day the DUTA General Body unconditionally withdrew the strike and resolved to return to work to fulfil their commitments to their students. Editorials appearing in the press the next day pointed out that DUTA had shown greater concern for the students than either the UGC or the Government.

One other incident which roused some controversy during the strike needs to be mentioned. Members of seven central trade unions had demonstrated their solidarity with DUTA by courting arrest in large numbers. While most teachers expressed appreciation and derived inspiration from this action, it was not uncommon to encounter the view, more so amongst women teachers, that it was not right to have working class organisations come out in our support. There was some distaste attached to the possible identification of DUTA with working class organisations.

In August 1986, the Democratic Teachers' Front (DTF) conducted a fund raising campaign in support of Delhi's striking textile workers. Trade Union representatives who had participated in the court arrest action went from college to college with DTF members. With few exceptions teachers donated generously. In fact, the response in some of the women's colleges was even better than in the men's colleges.

Conclusions

The relationship between DUTA and its women members as it developed after the Emergency and specifically since the perspective of united struggle gained predominance, has been a mutually beneficial one. The active role of women teachers in DUTA activities has influenced

DUTA's perspective on many issues and has become a significant measure of DUTA's strength. Similarly, the women. teachers have also gone through a process of radicalisation by participating in DUTA's struggles. They have redefined their roles and have become occupied with new issues. This has meant a raising of consciousness and I would not hesitate to define this as political consciousness.

Lessons can be drawn from DUTA's experience both by professional associations and by their women members and I hope this paper will be considered a contribution in this direction.

Chapter 11

Women Teachers of Tamil Nadu in Struggle

V. VASANTHI DEVI

V ery rarely have working women in middle class professions in India shown such militancy and risen against the State machinery in such unbelievably large numbers as did the women teachers of Tamil Nadu in the historic teachers' struggle of November-December 1985. The struggle raged for forty-two days and brought the state Government system presided over by the All India Anna Dravida Munnetra Kazagam (AIADMK) to a virtual standstill. It was a saga of epic proportions and became a milestone in the history of the trade union movement. The teachers of Tamil Nadu forged a rare and spectacular unity among themselves, bringing within their fold the entire teaching community of the state, from primary school to college levels, numbering around three and a half lakh. They rose against what they perceived to be gross injustices against them in terms of pay scales and service conditions and when repression was let loose against them and the Government resorted to coercion and intimidation, the struggle was turned into a virtual fight for civil rights. The women teachers, who form a significant proportion of the teaching community, rose along with the men, sometimes ahead of them, struck work and braved the police, courted arrest and went to prison in thousands. A rough estimate has placed the number of teachers in the prisons of the state at the height of the struggle at an incredible 60,000 with women forming what might seem a hyperbolic overestimate of 10,000. This paper attempts to study this struggle and I may be pardoned if, in an attempt to capture its heroic dimensions I overstep the restraint of language required of a research paper. I have made use of questionnaires and interviews to gather the material.

A Brief History of the Struggle

The teachers of Tamil Nadu are a long suffering lot, their pay scales among the lowest - 22nd place among the states of India - in the country. The Eighth Finance Commission had recommended that to bring the abominably low pay scales of Tamil Nadu teachers on par with the national average, they must be enhanced by a minimum of 25%. Expectations had been raised by the constitution of the Fourth Pay Commission, but its report was a shattering blow to the teachers. It had dismally failed to meet even a fraction of the teachers' demands.

Against such a background of bitterness and frustration, associations of different categories of teachers, from primary school to college levels, started coming together to form a federation called JACTTEA (Joint Action Council of Tamil Nadu Teachers' and Employees' Associations.) Starting with 4 Associations the umbrella widened to ultimately include a formidable 44 Associations. It is under this umbrella that the historic struggle was launched and JACTTEA became a sacred mantra to the teaching community.

It must be mentioned that the teachers' movement in Tamil Nadu does not have much of a militant history behind it. Except for a couple of school and college teachers' Associations, others had a very passive past and some were newly formed.

While programmes for mobilising teachers were being organised, the Government precipitated the flare up by a repressive step it took on November 3, 1985. When teachers in a large number of centres all over the state, had gathered on the day to burn the Government order that contained the unjust provisions of the Pay Commission, the police swooped down on them and arrested them. Hundreds of teachers were remanded to custody for 15 days and were thrown into prisons. The flash point was reached. From the next day teachers started pouring into the streets, demanding the release of their colleagues. Schools and colleges were paralysed. From November 7th a campaign was launched to fill the prisons and a call for indefinite strike was given.

The response from teachers was tremendous and far beyond the expectations of the leaders. Hundreds and thousands of teachers came out to picket and court arrest. The bravery and heroism displayed by them was incredible. Suddenly, the black pall of fear was lifted from their shouldeors. They could no longer be intimidated by the police, or the prisons on the courts. The timid, peace-loving and almost docile teaching community threw away its reservations and inhibitions.

The Government resorted to many coercive, repressive measures and unfair labour practices to intimidate the teachers. It came out with very expensive, long columns in newspapers every day denying the charges of the teachers and calling their demands unfair. The teaching community had no matching resources to deny them in similar columns; but in thousands of everyday meetings in the field of battle they were refuted. The Government advertised for recruits to fill the places of teachers who were on strike and gave an ultimatum that posts will be filled if teachers did not return to work. The teachers treated the ultimatum with disdain and not one returned to her post. When the month of November came to an end, teachers' salaries were withheld. This attempt to hit them below the belt resulted in further infuriating the teachers.

Tragic events followed. One teacher, Karuppahhan, died in prison, followed by sixteen others, who dropped dead while participating in the struggle programmes. Their martyrdom added fury to the fire.

A striking feature of the struggle was the solidarity extended to it by other trade unions throughout the period. The camaraderie reached its height with the struggle nearing its fortieth day, when all the major trade unions decided to call for a general strike, a very rare and exceptional gesture in trade union history. The proposed step struck fear in the hearts of the rulers, who were ultimately dragged to the negotiating table. An agreement was reached between the executive of the JACTTEA and the Chief Minister of Tamil Nadu. All cases registered against teachers were dropped; the principle of no-work no-pay was set aside and full salary was paid to teachers for all the 42 days of the struggle and the demands of the teachers were referred to a one-man Commission.

Women Teachers in the Struggle

The participation of women teachers throughout the period was intense and overwhelming. The barriers that confine middle class women were suddenly blown to pieces and they marched ahead of the men, formed long picket lines and became the nightmare of the police. At the height of the struggle, approximately 10,000 women were in prison. The prestige of the State Government received a shattering blow and it will take years for it to live down the shame it suffered by keeping women in prison.

Women participated in all the programmes of the struggle and embraced all its forms. They marched through the streets shouting slogans in frenzied voices, staged dharnas, sat down on the streets and blocked the traffic, fully participated in the strike, picketed and went to prison. They played a key role in mobilising other teachers and enlisting public support. In one district (Anna) a woman was fully in charge of the struggle and enjoyed unquestioned leadership. This was one of the two districts (the other being Madurai) from where women went to prison the earliest and stayed inside for the longest period, sometimes ranging upto 22 days.

During the festival of Diwali many women teachers were in jail. Diwali is perhaps the most important and joyous festival in the year, with a lot of sentiments attached to the togetherness of the family on the occasion and women's role is central to the celebrations. The scenes in the prisons on the day were touching, with families visiting the teachers with eatables, and children hugging mothers with tears in their eyes. But in the midst of such moving scenes one thing was clear - not one woman was prepared to leave the prison to share the joyous day with her family. More than tears, it was anger that flashed in those usually gentle eyes and they swore that the betrayal of the Government would not be forgotten or forgiven.

The participation of women teachers in the eighteen districts of Tamil Nadu was uneven. While in certain districts like Anna, Madurai, Coimbatore and Periyar, women's participation was very significant, in certain others it was totally negligible.

It is unfortunate that the movement has not properly kept records and it has not been possible to get the exact number of women who went to jail. The attempt made by the researcher to get the information from prison authorities has so far not succeeded. The reluctance of the authorities is due to the embarrassment in officially admitting the huge numbers arrested and secondly due to the recentness of the struggle and the still volatile situation of the teachers' movement. The data below is pieced together from newspaper accounts and is undoubtedly inaccurate and incomplete. The women were in prison for a period ranging from one day to 24 days; in the district of Coimbatore, for instance, from one day to 7 days; in Anna, from 3 to 22 days, with the largest number staying inside for 14 days.

Name of District	No. of men arrested	No. of women arrested	Total arrested
Tirunelveli	950	26	976
Ramnad	71	-	7
Pasumpen	1,653	71	1,724
Kamarajar	1,555	264	1,819
Madurai	4,744	1,086	5,830
Anna	1,944	449	2,393
Coimbatore	7,210	2,741	9,951
Nilgiris	426	65	491
Trichi	4,043	634	5,677
Erode	335	-	335
Salem	2,810	882	3,692
Dharmapuri	250	-	250
Thanjavur	2,270	18	2,288
S. Arcot	4,056	-	4,056
Madras	2,034	66	2,100
N. Arcot	16	-	16

Apart from those who were remanded to custody, there were a large number of women and men, who courted arrest but who were let off by the Government. Especially after the 21st of November, a demoralised Government with its prisons bursting at their seams, the prison administration on the brink of collapse, stopped remanding teachers to custody.

Findings of the Study

The method adopted for the study was a kind of purposive random sampling. Three hundred questionnaires were sent out with some allocation ensured to each of the 17 districts, to office bearers of important teachers' associations or those who were in charge of organising the struggle, with a request to distribute them to women teachers ensuring distribution in three categories: one, those who went to prison; two, those who did not go to prison but participated in other forms of struggle; and three, those who did not participate. Where it was possible for the researcher to get addresses of women teachers who participated in the struggle, questionnaires were individually mailed. Such addresses were available for three districts: Anna (the researcher's district), Tirunelveli and Madras. The first 75 responses received were taken for study.

The sample shows that out of the 75 respondents, 51 (a very high proportion) had gone to prison. The explanation could be that those who went to prison were the first to respond, as they had an understandable pride in their militancy and sacrifice. Of the other 24 in the sample, 6 had participated in picketing with the intention of courting arrest, but were not arrested by the authorities, as on certain days during the long struggle, they decided to just keep the teachers in police stations for a day, without remanding them to custody, and on certain others, specific instructions were given not to arrest women teachers; 9 had participated in the strike; 3 in processions and there were only 6 in the sample of 75 who had not participated in the struggle in any form. A serious limitation imposed by such a skewed sample is that a comparative study of participants and non-participants to isolate the variables that spark such militancy is not possible.

The district-wise distribution of the 75 respondents is as follows: Anna - 31; Tirunelveli - 16; Madras - 2; Trichy - 1; Periyar - 1; Kamarajar - 5; Coimbatore - 6; Salem - 4; South Arcot - 1. The very high representation of Anna district is due, one, to its being the researcher's district and the proximity of teachers enabled frequent reminders and second, it was one of the few districts where women's participation was very high. Unfortunately, it has not been possible, from our study to establish why women's participation is so uneven among the different districts.

Distribution of the respondents into urban-rural categories shows that 14 of them come from rural areas, while 56 come from urban areas. It is, however, not clear whether small towns that were not very different from rural areas were also included in the urban category. Of the 14 teachers from rural areas, 12 had been to jail, while 37 of the 56 in urban areas had similarly distinguished themselves.

Of the 75 teachers, 40 were in Government, Municipal and Panchayat schools while 35 came from private management schools.

The feature seems to contradict the generally held belief that private managements hold their teachers, especially women teachers, in utter repression, at times in conditions of near bondage. A strange and notable feature of the struggle was the unprecedented encouragement and active support it received from private managements, especially minority, Christian managements.

Forty six of the respondents came from exclusively women's institutions while 29 were from co-educational schools. Out of the 46 teachers from exclusively women's schools 28 had been to prison, while 23 out of the 29 from co-educational institutions had. The above figures negate the general belief that women's schools are pools of conservatism that perpetuate a semi-feudal ethos while a more liberal atmosphere prevails in co-educational institutions. This aspect is closely linked to the unusual support the struggle received from private managements, as most of the women's schools are privately managed.

The teachers in the sample are fairly well distributed among the different categories: Primary school - 20; Middle school - 18; High school - 4; Higher secondary school - 11; and College - 22. Those who went to prison work out to: 17 out of 20 Primary, 13 out of 18 Middle, 1 out of 4 High school, 7 out of 11 Higher secondary and 13 out of 22 college level teachers. Fourteen out of the 22 college teachers came from one women's college. This college had stood in the forefront of the struggle, with 25 teachers bravely courting arrest and remaining in prison for 14 days.

Does marriage, with its domestic responsibilities and care of children act as a big constraint on women joining militant movements? Not in times of big upsurge, when there is a need to rally together. This is proved by the sample, where 63 of the 75 respondents are married, yet 44 of them went to prison and 6 were involved in picketing. Of the 12 unmarried women, 7 went to prison.

Nor does the thought of leaving children, especially little ones, uncared for at home dampen women's militancy. In the sample, of the 44 married women who went to prison, 42 had children -- 5 of them had children below 5 years; 2 had big families with 6 to 9 children and 7 had more than 4 children. And yet they forgot their motherly cares and rose to the occasion.

The age-wise distribution shows that no one was below 25 years. Perhaps, youth, at least among middle class, employed women, does not encourage tendencies to militancy and daring. At a young marriageable age, girls having gone to prison is likely to be considered a terrible stigma that will ruin their chances of getting married. It is also possible that the younger teachers are new entrants in their jobs, and their services are not regularised and thus the risk of losing their jobs is all the more serious. The largest number, 52, belonged to the middle age group - 36 to 50. Six of them were above 50 years, of whom 3 were on the verge of retirement. The three are not likely to benefit directly out of the struggle. They mentioned that they were aware of the fact, but still went to prison because they wanted the younger teachers and generations of teachers to benefit by their sacrifice.

Did all these women, especially the ones who went to prison, have a long schooling in trade unionism through membership in teachers' associations? At the time the struggle flared up, a large number of teachers in the state did not belong to any of the 44 teachers' associations that had federated to form JACTTEA. But, the struggle was so compulsive and all pervasive and its emotional impact so intense that teachers were swept into it without being mediated by associations. The spontaneity witnessed at the grassroots was touching and often unbelievable. The sample bears this out: 12 of those jailed did not belong to any teachers' association and had neither organisational training nor any leadership structure that could mobilise them for the struggle. The distribution of teachers among associations is as follows (the figure in brackets shows the number that went to prison): Primary School Teachers' Association 1 - 16 (16): Primary School Teachers' Association II - 4(2); Primary School Teachers' Association III - 3(2); Middle School Teachers' Association - 7(5); B.T. Teachers' Association - 4(1); P.G. Teachers' Association - 2(0); Tamil Nadu Government Collegiate Teachers' Association - 20(13); Madurai University Teachers' Association - 2(0). The first association of Primary school teachers was the most militant during the struggle. Of the others, members of the Government Collegiate Teachers' Association and Middle School Teachers' Association courted arrest in large numbers.

It is a well known and a rightly lamented fact that women are rarely seen in leadership position in trade unions. In our sample of 75, twenty-three had held positions of office bearers; but except for 3, others had held their posts within their own college/school, mainly women's units. One had held the post of secretary of her town level association; one, that of district treasurer; one, of zonal joint secretary. Of these 23 office-bearers, 17 had been to prison; one had participated in picketing and 4 in the strike.

Were there certain exceptional provocations that triggered such rare militancy among middle class women? What were the reasons that impelled the women to such militancy? The largest number of them, 68, have cited the injustices of the Pay Commission, its discrimination against teachers as the major reason. The 'movement spirit' of the teachers and their 'commitment to the cause' came a close second with 58 respondents; forty-eight stated that they were provoked by the repressive measures of the Government of swooping down on teachers and throwing them in prison. Another sizeable number, 45, said that the dedicated and tireless working of certain leaders inspired them. A few, 23, have given reasons like the involvement of fellow teachers, the support of the husband or other family members or of the management.

What had been the attitude of the nearest kin, especially the husband, to the active participation of women and to their militancy like courting arrest? In the close-knit family system that prevails in our society, the stand taken by family members could be a crucial factor. A sizeable number of our respondents who went to prison - 30, had the strong support of their husbands; 8 husbands had extended moderate support; 9 were indifferent, while 2 were opposed. Strangely, none had stated that they faced severe opposition from their husbands.

In our sample, 11 women had teacher husbands. Of them 9 had been to prison. Two of them had been to prison, while their husbands stayed home. Seven teacher couples had both braved the prison, leaving their children behind to be looked after by mothers in 3 cases, mothers-in-law in 2 cases, by sister in one and by a colleague in another.

Many teachers have referred to the loving support given by their husbands by taking the responsibility and care of the children and family. Some husbands had worked day and night to mobilise other teachers and organise solidarity action among the unions they belonged to. Some husbands had been a source of inspiration to their wives and had encouraged them to stay in jails for as long as necessary. Some were ideologically committed to the path of struggle and had been instrumental in bringing their wives to it. Some were believers in women's rights and full equality of sexes, which they said, should be proved in the arena of struggle. A couple of them had joined their wives and other teachers in the rally held in Madras after the struggle.

All the parents were not so supportive, however. Twelve had extended strong support, 13 moderate support, 15 were indifferent, while 3 opposed their participation in the struggle. Once again, in no case had parents strongly opposed the bold step taken by their daughters.

Among relatives, in 16 cases strong support had been extended; 16 were indifferent while a larger number had opposed. A sizeable number of respondents - 22- had received very strong support from friends, many of whom were likely to be fellow teachers.

A crucial factor was the stand taken by the management. One would expect that managements would join hands with the Government and oppose the struggle and use their power to prevent teachers from joining the struggle. It was no doubt true in certain cases, but a strange factor that was important during the struggle was the full support extended by private managements to the struggling teachers. In our sample, in 12 cases private managements had extended strong support, 6 moderate support, 7 were indifferent, 4 had opposed and 5 strongly opposed. In a few instances, managements, especially minority Christian managements had conducted mass and blessed teachers who were courting arrest. The managements had supplied food to their teachers in jails all the 14 or more days they were inside. The families were looked after in certain other cases. When the Government withheld the salaries of the teachers for the month they were on strike, many managements paid them out of their own coffers. All through the period of the struggle, they had offered their school premises and other facilities for organising meetings, etc.

It is likely that many of the women who courted arrest did so in a momentary impulse triggered by the upsurge. If that were the case, once behind bars, in a world dark, alien and fearsome, did they regret the step they had taken? What were their feelings while in prison? An overwhelming number, 49 of the 51 who went to prison, did not regret the momentous decision they had taken; forty-six felt positively proud and elated at their decision; forty-eight felt that their spirit of involvement and commitment to the cause and the movement had increased while in prison and 47 were hopeful that the struggle will end in victory and their courage and sacrifice will not be in vain.

The prison experiences related by the respondents bring out their bravery, dedication, faith in the cause and immense pride and involvement in the movement. Some say the experience was intense, beautiful and elevating. The solidarity they felt with other teachers in and out of prison was the highest point in their lives. It was a glorious experience to some, who vow they are prepared to go through the same experience and offer themselves to the cause again and again. Many had felt that a larger number of women should have courted arrest and that the success of the movement lay in teachers' maintaining their historic unity. Only one teacher said she would never like to go through the experience again.

Women members of their respective trade unions are rarely members of women's organisations. Those who struggle for pay increases and better service conditions in their professional fields, often do not, at the same time, join the struggle for women's rights. What is the linkage between the two that emerges from our sample? Only 11 respondents of our sample were members of women's organisations; but 17 had participated in the women's movement; sixty-four of them definitely felt the need for such a movement; out of them 62 felt that women teachers must participate in the women's movement; however, a slightly smaller number, 54, said they would join it.

What about the future? If the struggle erupts again, will these heroines rise in similar waves of righteous indignation, brave Government coercion and repression and fill the prisons? In our sample, except for one, all the others said that they would participate in future struggles; thirty-five of them said that their future involvement will be full, intense and active, while 31 would be moderately involved. Is it because the euphoria of the struggle has not yet faded? Not likely, as the questionnaires were administered eight months after the struggle was over. So, it is not a freak outburst of militancy among women teachers. They have considered their commitment to struggle and will provide a militant cadre for the future movement.

Conclusion

The women teachers' struggle in Tamil Nadu is undoubtedly an extraordinary episode, a glorious instance of middle class women rising in intense militancy. What are the inferences one could draw from it? How replicable is the experience in future trade union movements? It is very difficult to answer these questions with mild assurance. The element of contingency is strong. Nevertheless, one could venture to say that in moments of great upsurge, women in middle class professions would cross the barriers imposed by their class and culture and would become a brave fighting force. The struggle had strong moral overtones throughout and it is likely that this was a crucial contributing factor to the uprising of women. The gains won must now be consolidated by systematic, conscious and far-sighted planning.

The heroic struggle was withdrawn after 42 days, accepting the constitution of a one-man Commission. After a long wait of nine months, the Commissions' report has been submitted to the Government. The Government however, has not cared to disclose the report. A few measly concessions based on the Commission's recommendations are all that have been so far granted. The teaching community in the state rightly considers that the attitude of the Government is a betrayal of and an affront to a historic struggle. Mobilising is on for the next stage of the struggle. What would it be like? Would women teachers once again rally to the call when it comes?

Chapter 12

Informalism in a Gender Setting: Strategies and Counter-Strategies

P.M. MATHEW

Introduction

T he emergence of a movement of working class women is not a unilinear process. The necessary and sufficient objective conditions for it vary according to time, space and the specificity of social production. The subordination of labour to capital and its historical specificity is central to capitalist development, as is the development of class-consciousness among labour and the specificity of class struggle. These among other objective conditions, influence and shape a historically and spatially specific form of social production, including that of the so-called 'informal sector'. In this paper we shall draw upon the specific evidence of Kerala.

The essence of the theory, strategy and the tactics of women's liberation in the context of class struggle is their conscious political organisation (along with men) to realise this goal. This may be visualised at three levels; a) class; b) gender; and c) the interaction of the two at the organisational and ideological levels.

Viewed from this angle, there are two broad phases in the history of the women's movement in Kerala: a) the pre-1950 period - during which a radical movement, concentrating on political activity emerged; and b) the post-1950 period which may be described as the institutional phase. In the latter phase, radical women's organisations have been left with the task of exposing the depoliticisation strategy behind women's welfare schemes and the political-ideological functions it had hitherto been performing. In Kerala, such schemes have been implemented both by the Government and by various religious communities and caste groups. While the "success" and "failure" of the women's movement in this regard is a matter of debate, it is important to examine the strategies and counter-strategies under different historical settings. This paper is an attempt to examine the reaction of various women's organisations in Kerala in relation to employment strategies in the 'informal sector'.

An understanding of the dynamics of the informal sector is vital for academicians and activists alike. The problems as well as the potential inherent in it are compounded as gender is introduced as an added dimension.

The conventional neo-dualist school links the two sectors, formal and informal, in a benign relationship and speaks of the 'integration of women in development' as a means of their 'emancipation'. These social scientists argue that, generally the participation of women in economic activities is unsatisfactory and its level should be raised so that women may contribute to and get fully integrated with economic development.[1]

The Petty Commodity Production (PCP) school advocates increasing autonomy of petty commodity producers, and consequently the informal sector. A logical extension of their argument would stand for a policy obverse to that of the neo-dualists. In both cases there are conflicting a priori theoretical assumptions.

The "informal sector" has often also been viewed by academicians as a phenomenon of the 1970s. However, its origins may be traced to the history of capitalism itself. Capitalism has always maintained a variety of forms of production in order to appropriate and accumulate surplus. These forms have also often been tailored to the existing social institutions and political relationships, both formal and informal, and by and large, they reflect the socio-political reality of the times.

Shift to Welfare

The 1930s and 1940s saw a remarkable upsurge of peasants' and workers' movements in various parts of India, in which women also played an active role. This historical experience is the background of the major shifts in activity of organisations such as the All-India Women's Conference (AIWC), the Congress Mahila Sangh, the NCWI, and the YWCA in the early post-independence period.

Prior to the mid-1940s, these organisations were an expression of the so called women's 'equality movement'; now there was a shift to social welfare. They began to take up rural and poor-women based welfare programmes, and began to promote village level 'a political' women's groups called mahila samajams (or mahila-mandals).

These developments, in fact, meant a rejuvenation of the traditional organisations of women. The mahila samajams further got official sanction under the First Five Year Plan.[2]

Gradually, more and more private programmes and the organisations behind them began to get official sanction. This ushered in an era of institutionalised and bureaucratised women's welfare programmes. A pyramidal bureaucratic and administrative structure, with the Central Social Welfare Board at the apex and the local-level mahila mandals at the base emerged. According to the data available with the Central Social Welfare Board, 34.55 per cent of the mahila samajams had been started during the period 1951-60.[3]

Welfare programmes and the women's organisations themselves became bureaucratised, and their real control continued to be with a group of elite women as in the past. Soon the weaker sections of society got disillusioned with such organisations. This coincided with the re-emergence of the Communist Party and its mass organisations (which had gone underground as a result of a ban on them) and the formation of the pro-CPI(M) Kerala Mahila Federation (KMF). The struggles of weaker sections, especially of workers of coir and cashew industries, witnessed a boom with greater women's participation.

The official thrust of women's co-operatives after the early 1960s was possibly a policy reaction to this women's mass participation. The shift in emphasis from gender-neutral to all-women co-operatives was essentially a proposition of elite women and their organisations. However, the co-operatives thus formed were a replica of the mahila samajams which had already degenerated and stagnated. Samajams which were engaged in activities such as tailoring, running of nursery schools, etc., were now transformed into co-operatives.

Welfare to Employment

These earlier developments are the background against which the interest after the early 1970s in the informal sector and specifically in the role of women in this sector should be viewed. The literature and policies relating to women after the 1970s show ideological overtones of the emerging interest of capital in women's organisations as a potential gold mine of cheap labour. One argument put forward was that the level of women's work participation is unsatisfactory, so policy should aim at raising this level so that women may be fully integrated in economic development.[4] Economic development, for them generally means growth in per capita gross domestic product so; in order to contribute to it women have to be engaged in what they called 'economic' or 'gainful' activity.[5]

Inherent in the above argument is the view that women's development is essentially an economic problem, though its social and political aspects are also admitted. It deals with the social and political aspects by simply reserving certain areas exclusively for women.

Though the new thinking on women's economic emancipation is apparently more progressive, in reality it is retrogressive. Since early 1950s oppressed women (especially rural women) have been viewed as a potential source of revolt and have been offered programmes on a marginal scale such as nutrition information, maternal and child care and some employment and training programmes. Of late, programmes dealing with and reinforcing women's reproductive and child-rearing roles have also been called wasteful as they do not raise the 'economic productivity' of women. This reflects a news shift in emphasis from welfare to employment.

This shift has also meant rationalising the massive exploitation and abject poverty that the so called informal sector characterises. By attributing a benign character to the relationship between the formal and informal sectors, the exploitation of women is attributed to inadequate sectoral integration, also implying that women's productive employment depends upon the needs of the organised formal sector.

Ancillarisation as Co-operativisation

The early attempts at forming women's co-operatives in the 'informal sector' were only a partial success. The Third Five Year Plan period, however witnessed a spurt in the number of co-operatives, and they were viewed as instruments of arresting the potential upsurge of radical ideas among working class women. Today when large industry is ancillarising and expanding the socalled informal sector they have assumed a new role, that of an instrument of integrating women into the capitalist system. The constant efforts of both the Central and State Governments have brought about a virtual boom in the number of co-operatives in the post-1975 period.

The greater ancillarisation of women's productive ventures and their connection with the large-scale enterprises, indicates a greater integration of the destinies of working class women and their organisations with the interest of the Indian capitalist class, which collaborates with its international counterpart. Though studies in the context of women-sponsored enterprises are few, various regional studies have shown directional imbalances in the flow of output and income from the large-scale to the small-scale units[6] and that there often exists a tendency towards a pathological dependence on imported technology and continuous labour-displacement.

The economic activities of these organisations also witnessed a qualitative change; from running tailoring schools, making papad and other food materials, to ready-made garments, handicrafts and processing of modern food items like squashes, pickles, etc., mainly for the national and international market. In the pre-1970s production and marketing were largely autonomous decisions of the women's enterprises; now they have become largely dependent upon the needs of parent firms.

Some women's organisations changed their previous activities. Others not earlier engaged in any productive activities, started them and established linkages with their own parent firms. Some of the products were merely sold by the parent firm, but for many other products, only the limited role of assembling the products was left to the woman's organisations by the parent firms.

What specific role did co-operatives play in relation to employment of female labour? It may be argued that cheap labour could be recruited otherwise also since the market for unskilled and semi-skilled labour in Kerala is a buyers' market. Direct recruitment and employment of labour by the capitalist however, involves risk, firstly, that of unionisation. Moreover, for monopoly capital, which operates at the national-international level, direct employment creates diseconomies, which are absent in the case of indirect employment, for example, through a women's organisation.

In the early 1970s women's organisations also changed their strategy from that of engaging in a multitude of activities to only a single activity. This increased during the post-1977 period. Specialisation has obvious economic advantages in terms of economies of scale and their effective use. However, in the case of ancillaries, this specialisation is more conducive to the interest of the parent firms, as the latter can dictate the price and the quality of the product. The emerging phenomenon thus has been the specialisation in the production/assembling of products for the international market. Electronics, handicrafts and ready-made garments are some such items in which many women's production units have been specialising. The best example of such a phenomenon has been KELTRON's linkages with its ancillaries.

International spokesmen of the capitalist path of development are increasingly projecting the Newly Industrialising Countries' (NICs) inescapable 'integration with the developed capitalist world' as the best examples of capitalist development. And in those countries certain projects assisted substantially by international capital are being projected as "success" stories.

KELTRON has been one such "success" story. Similarly, in a situation where most co-operatives face severe problems as business entities, the KELTRON-ancillaries are being projected as 'successful'. This projection has the potential of creating illusions in the minds of unemployed women leading to the setting up of a network of co-opera|ives.

The reality, however, is very different. For instance, since technical training, quality control and sale of finished products are all handled by KELTRON itself, development of skills and leadership qualities is blocked for the co-operators. Moreover, the co-operatives are, though democratically constituted, for all practical purposes, extremely controlled because of their forward national/international linkages.

The latest devlopments in public policy relating to women's organisations are attempts to reorganise the Mahila Samajams in tune with the Sixth Five Year Plan document. The Plan highlights the role of women-preferred industries and states that a gradual process of mechanisation should be thought of in traditional industries where the majority of women are currently employed.

The latest thinking of the Government of Kerala revolves around a package deal for Mahila Samajams which involves a target group approach, the logical corollary of which is a viability criterion.[7] Mahila

Samajams are proposed to be made least voluntary in character. Selected samajams will be supported by official sources like the UNICEF, the Government and by the business establishments on condition that they will engage only in 'viable' activities chalked out for them.

Exclusive dependence on a 'cheap labour' hypothesis however, can be misleading. The social reality of the post-1977 period is complex. There was a substantial increase in the number of political organisations of women and various other interest groups. All the political parties which had no women's wings so far, took the initiative to set them up. Organisations such as the Mahila Congress intensified their activities. The Mahila Federation was replaced by a national organisation called All India Democratic Women's Association (AIDWA). The Revolutionary Socialist Party (RSP) took the initiative to form an All Kerala Women's Organisation, the Kerala Aikya Mahila Sangham (KAMS).

Another notable development in this period has been the emerging unity and cohesion among the pro-left organisations. The changed political climate since 1979, in which the Left Democratic Front (LDF) was formed, has led to a realignment of forces on the women's front too. An example is the formation of the National Campaign Committee of Trade Unions (NCCTU), and other coordination committees of women's organisations favouring CPI, CPI(M) and RSP.

Caste/Religion and Gender

Caste and religion are not politically neutral. The recent intervention of international capitalism in women's organisations has been circuitous; in it caste and religious institutions play an instrumental role.

Hence the relevance of the following two developments: a) the establishment of the social welfare organisations by caste/religious groups; and b) the active interest taken by these highly centralised organisations to sponsor and/or support other organisations, such as women's co-operatives, registered societies, often called 'social centres' and/or Mahila Samajams, at the local level. The Nair Service Society (NSS) and the Muslim Education Society (MES) set up their central women's organisations, and the SNDP Yogam intensified the activities of its women's wing during the post-1977 period. The Christian Churches which had been engaged in various social service activities, began co-ordinating them under single diocese-level umbrellas named variously as Development Societies, Social Service Societies, etc., which, in turn, sponsored local-level organisations serviced by their central pool of funds mostly obtained from foreign sources. It is notable that 76.71 per cent of the total social centres existing in 1984 were started in the post-1976 period.

Being the pioneers in forming charity-oriented women's organisations as early as the late 19th century, these groups turned to Mahila Samajams by the mid-1960s and to women's co-operatives by the mid-1970s. Most of these organisations and their production centres are attached to churches, convents and orphanages, the workers being drawn from orphans, widows and children of poor families of the communities concerned. These organisations together perform the following functions: 1) supply cheap labour; 2) marketing of products (for balwadi equipments, sewing machines for tailoring schools, etc.); and 3) depoliticisation.

That there is a concentration of women workers in the informal sector of most developing countries, makes it necessary to examine the interaction of economic processes and dominant ideologies in the structuring and allocation of spaces to women.[9] KELTRON's intervention should be viewed in the light of international fragmentation of the labour process which has led to differential employment of women at different stages of their life cycle. In the present phase of this process, certain industries have relocated certain aspects of their production to the Third World, especially those parts which offer the most advantage in terms of exploitation of cheap labour.[10] Caste and religion act as connecting links in this emerging process.

A Look at an Informal Sector

In Kerala, there are a large number of small-scale units registered under the District Industries Centre engaged in the manufacture of dipped goods, such as rubber bands, finger caps and rubber thread. Most of these units are concentrated in the suburbs of Kottayam, a small town in Central Kerala. The dipped-goods industry employs about 4,500 workers, of which 94 per cent are women; and of these, 91.2 per cent are less than twenty years old.[11]

The important manufacturing activities involved in this industry are dipping, cutting and drying, which do not require considerable skills. Nevertheless, the workers have been categorised into permanent, temporary and casual, according to their linkages with the entrepreneur. All women workers are employed on a daily-wage basis, but permanent workers get regular employment under a single employer. The others work irregularly and under different employers at different times. Most women workers, though they have worked continuously for a number of years, are still considered 'temporary'.

Relations prevalent in the industry may broadly be described as feudal. Workers are often selected from households in neighbourhoods near-by. In an essentially rural setting, the social and family status of the entrepreneurs basically influences the specifity of the labour-capital relationship. The entrepreneurs further reinforce it by establishing rapport with political parties and caste-communal organisations, creating for themselves a new identity.

Family background is a crucial factor on the labour front also. The relationship of the employers with the women workers is indirect. That employment in this industry is clearly demarcated for unmarried women (who are virtually controlled by their parents), makes it easier for employers to establish a direct relation with the parents rather than with the women workers themselves. This makes the women a third party and weakens their bargaining power. Besides, the young age of the women workers limits their mobility and chances of interaction with other workers in other units, creating information barriers. Moreover, even their parents consider them subsidiary earners merely supplementing the income of the family until marriage.[12]

For these reasons, the capitalists can rely exclusively on the labour of unmarried women who are thrown out of employment as soon as they are married. Under the contract labour system,[13] the worker at least has the potential of organising against the employer and contractor. Here parents or some workers themselves assume the role of the contractor.

This is also reflected in the wage structure. While the average rate in the industry is Rs. 5.80, and the maximum rate Rs. 10, the average for women is only Rs. 3.

The web of exploitative mechanisms is reinforced and nurtured by apolitical ideologies and political, caste and communal platforms are often used. In 87.5 per cent of the factories studied it is common practice for employers to distribute gifts at the time of the local feasts and festivals. It is also common practice to distribute cakes during Christmas. Similarly, when women workers get married, the employers give them a wedding gift and at the same time retrench them.

Counter-strategies

Evolution of appropriate political strategies relating to labour, demands a correct understanding of the existing political matrix. When gender is introduced as an additional variable, the matrix becomes much more complex.

The pro-CPI(M) All India Democratic Women's Association (AIDWA) and the pro-CPI Kerala Mahila Sangham (KMS) rightly consider women's organisations as one means of politicisation in the march towards a classless society, which alone will change suppressive family structures leading to women's liberation.[14] The pro-RSP Kerala Aikya Mahila Sangham (KAMS) on the other hand, focuses on the economic aspect of women's liberation both in terms of its stated objectives and in practice. Nevertheless, all radical organisations have to trade off direct political action and politicisation against offering/ participating in economic programmes. Exclusive concentration on the former leads the movement away from the concrete reality of practical politics, preoccupation with the latter sets apolitical politics in motion.

At least two organisations, KMS and AIDWA, organise and participate in working women's struggles, especially in the traditional industries such as coir, cashew, handloom, etc., and in the agricultural sector. In the past, these organisations were regional in character and could devote time and energy to local political issues. Of late, with the formation of national-level organisations, they have to raise national issues such as price rise, oppressive legislation, etc., as well as engage in local level economic programmes for women. This widening of the dimensions of the women's question has apparently created an incompatibility between political mobilisation and economic action. This may possibly be the crucial reason for the apparent regression in the women's movement cited by some social scientists.[15]

A mass organisation, compared to a political one, has only a limited chance of political action. The former has an edge over the latter in terms of organising particular sections of society on a wider canvas of economic and social demands, which may in turn, contribute to politicisation. The acid test of the success of any such organisation lies in how effectively this function is performed.

These organisations are relatively active in the traditional industries and in the agricultural sector; whereas in the other industries their activity has not been satisfactory. All the three radical organisations

AIDWA, KMS and KAMS are trying their best to give maximum possible economic benefits to their members by making use of their goodwill and through representation in various administrative bodies. This is relatively easy. However, they have not been successful enough in capturing the specificy of apolitical politics, i.e. the apolitical ideologies and strategies involved in the various economic programmes. Combining politicisation and economism is a difficult task where the level of class-consciousness among workers has not reached a basic minimum level as shown in the Kottayam example. Small attempts towards unionisation of women workers have taken place in the past but have failed miserably. It is these failed attempts that breed inertia among the workers. A plausible way to break this vicious circle may be cultural action.

The Imperative for Cultural Action

The term cultural action[16] has been used here in a specific context. The solution often cited in such situations has been greater conscientisation of workers. This over-used concept has a deceptive simplicity and the aura of a 'patron-client' relationship. Patron-client relationship however, will not lead to liberation of women workers. What is needed is greater participation. Women workers are aware of the various forms of exploitation they are subjected to. What is really lacking is the material conditions which enable such awareness to be transformed into concrete action.

　Kerala has a unique history of a strong　People's Science Movement (Kerala Shastra Sahitya Parishad) and a People's Art Movement (Kerala People's Art Club). Unfortunately, these movements too have of late started finding easy solutions to social problems. Can one think of a Perestroika, at least in the case of such popular movements? Moving along with the slogans of the time is easy; but interpreting an array of social problems in the light of developments in science and technology, institutional changes, tastes of the people, etc., is a challenging task. By reinterpreting theory as well as action on those lines alone can we find meaningful solutions to the gender issues in development.

NOTES AND REFERENCES

1.   See Dandekar, V.M., *Integration of Women in Economic Development*, EPW 17(44), October 1982.

2.   The First Five Year Plan document specifically emphasised that "... what is needed are a large number of voluntary workers ready to execute simple, well-thought out programmes in every village and locality." (Government of India (GOI) Planning Commission (1953): *First Five Year Plan*, Delhi, the Manager of Publications, GOI, p. 40).

3.   Mathew, P.M., and Nair, M.S., *Women's Organisations and Women's Interests*, New Delhi, Ashish Publishing House (1986).

4.   Dandekar (1982) op. cit.

5.   Dandekar (1982) op.cit.; Joshi, H., *Prospects and Case for Employment of Women in Indian Cities*, EPW, Special Number; August 1976; Mitra, Ashok, *Participation of Women in Socio-Economic Development: Indicators as Tools for Development Planning - The Case of India in* United Nations (1981).

6.   Kashyap, S.P., and Alagh, Y.K., *Structure of Gujarat Economy: Inter-Industry Flows at Producers' Prices, 1964-65*, Sardar Patel Institute of Economic and Social Research, Ahmedabad, 1971.

7.   Mathew, P.M., and Nair, M.S., op.cit.

8.   Mathew, P.M., and Nair, M.S.; op.cit.

9.   Heyzer, N., *Towards a Framework of Analysis*, IDS Bulletin 12(3), July 1981.

10. Elson D., and Pearson, K., *The Latest Phase of Internationalisation of Capital and Its Implications for Women in the Third World*, IDS Discussion Paper No. 150, Sussex, 1981.

11. These are tentative results drawn from a survey conducted in March-April 1986.

12. The majority of the workers were found to be aware of the exploitation to which they were subject to in terms of lower wages, working conditions and health hazards. However, they were found to be reluctant even to express discontentment. This was not only because of the fear of retrenchment, but also because of the pressure from the family. The parents often viewed such exploitation as transitory since the worker would normally lose employment on marriage.

13. This system prevailed in various forms in various traditional industries. 'Moopans' in coir and cashew industries and 'Kankanis' in plantations performed the function of recruiting adequate labour.

14. The objectives as stated in the Constitution of both the organisations centre around the following points: (a) to politicise working and middle class women in such a way as to attract them to the communist movement; (b) to educate them in order to make them capable of

fighting against superstitions and reactionary customs and practices; (c) to intervene effectively whenever womanhood is insulted and (d) to prepare them to participate in the struggle against the capitalist social order.

15. Kamat, A.R., *Women's Education and Social Change in India,* Social Scientist 5(1), August 1986, for instance, points out that there is evidence for a definite regression at the ideological level with inevitable consequences for social practice as compared to the radical thrust of the pre-independence period. According to him, a large majority of the new generation of educated women appear to be willing victims of this ideological regression and setback. The elite leadership of most organisations seems to prefer to work for official schemes under official patronage rather than to organise them on their local, sectional or common interests. For a detailed discussion of this point see Mathew and Nair (1986: 13-9).

16. For a discussion of this concept, see my discussion piece entitled *"Cultural Action Not Class Neutral",* Economic and Political Weekly, 22(7), 1987.

Chapter 13

Women in Trade Unions: A Study of AITUC, INTUC and CITU in the Seventies

Nivedita Menon

T he number of women in trade unions forms a small percentage of the total number of working women in India. Yet it is important to study their struggles, their participation in trade union activety and the extent to which trade union in turn are sensitive to political issues arising out of gender. The crucial role that trade unions play in struggles to transform unequal relations of power should place them in a position which makes them specially responsive to the double load of oppression borne by women workers in a capitalist society. This paper considers whether trade unions are in fact responsive to this issue. Three trade unions are studied, the All India Trade Union Congress (AITUC), the Indian National Trade Union Congress (INTUC) and the Centre of Indian Trade Unions (CITU). These are the three largest unions in India: AITUC·with a membership of 18 lakh affiliated to the Communist Party of India (CPI), INTUC with a membership of 33 lakh to the Congress (I) and CITU with a membership of 15 lakh to the Communist Party of India (Marxist) (CPI(M)).[1]

These trade unions have been studied on the basis of their weekly journals, INTUC's 'Indian worker', AITUC's 'Trade Union Record', CITU's 'Working Class' and 'Voice of the Working Women', and some pamphlets produced by these unions on specific issues. Thus the data base of this study is limited. At the same time, it is sufficient to draw certain legitimate generalisations of a preliminary nature. Also the focus on trade union membership particularly of three specific unions, will necessarily exclude the struggles of women workers who are not trade union membes. Hence it is necessary to be constantly aware of the limited field this study encompasses.

This paper attempts to study the perceptions of class struggle and patriarchy of AITUC, INTUC and CITU. The issue of equal pay for equal work is studied as a reliable indicator of the position of women within the trade union movement. This is done with particular reference to the views of AITUC, INTUC and CITU.

Women Workers and Trade Unions in India

It is not uncommon to find, in books titled 'Trade Unions and Politics in India' or 'Trade Union Movement in India', no reference to women workers. Where women are acknowledged at all, their low rates of participation in trade union activity are attributed to 'apathy'. This apathy has been explained by Mathur and Mathur, as due to women being more uneducated and illiterate than men, owing to the bonds of religion and social traditions and to the pressure of domestic responsibilities.[2] Since these reasons are very commonly put forward to explain why women are less active in trade unions than men, it is worthwhile exploring the ideological presuppositions which underlie them. To begin with, illiteracy as a factor inhibiting trade union membership is a contentious one. If its negative effects were strong, there ought to have been maximum unionisation and militancy among white collar workers. Such is not however the case. Hence, to attribute the lower participation of women to illiteracy is to leave unquestioned the patriarchal attitudes and structures which inhibit their participation and keep them illiterate in the first place. As to the bonds of religious and social traditions, it is true that women because of their role in the family and in the socialization of children do internalize such traditions to a greater degree than men. However, men are not free of such traditions either, and if their inhibitions can be broken down by a strong trade union movement, so can those of women. That women workers are still bound by such traditions (if they are) only points to the lesser degree to which the trade union movement has mobilised them.

A study of women employed in mines, carried out by the Labour Bureau of the Indian Government in 1979 found that 55 per cent of the women were ignorant about legislative provisions meant for their welfare.[3] This, in spite of the fact that women in the sample formed 13 per cent of the membership of trade unions, when their percentage to the total number of women sampled was 16 per cent. This shows a relatively high degree of trade union membership, but evidently the unions had not educated their women members about their rights. Disinterest on the part of trade unions then, is as responsible for the low membership of women as 'apathy' on the part of women. One study has shown that while in Ahmedabad women are the most loyal members of the Textile Labour Association (TLA), the TLA colluded with the Ahmedabad Mill Owners' Association to retrench female workers in the 1920s.[4]

Domestic responsibilities certainly inhibit women's participation in union activity, but the effort should be directed at questioning this sexual division of labour. There has however been no attempt at such a questioning either by the trade union movement or by studies of this movement.

Such studies fail to derive a correct picture also because they survey women workers alone. For instance, Nilima Acharya's study of the Jamshedpur branch of Life Insurance Employees showed that women union members took part only to the extent of attending meetings in times of crisis or joining processions for a charter of demands.[5] However, she has provided no information about the degree of participation of male members; it is quite probable that a majority of men too were only active to this degree.

Mathur and Mathur also go into the reasons why employment of women for wages outside the home "is not desirable and is not conducive to national and family prosperity."[6] That is, "the effects of lack of maternal care on the development of a child's personality.... The increasing number of still-born children, abortions, miscarriages.... in western countries...." Of course, this book was written twenty years ago, but this kind of attribution of the domestic sphere as natural to women is by no means an extinct attitude. A special article on women and the Indian labour movement in INTUC's journal *Indian Worker* during International Women's Year notes that the Indian trade union movement is being run by and large through gate meetings and by presenting cases in Industrial Courts and Tribunals. However, "it is difficult for women workers to address gate meetings where workers of one shift are going to the factory and those from the others coming out. It is also difficult for them to prove their worth before the Labour Courts and Tribunals because of the time and strain that preparation of a case entails."[7] Since it is not specified why exactly these activities are "difficult" for women, one must assume the author is referring to some natural delicacy in women and to their having to shoulder the entire responsibility of household work. This last is, of course, assumed to be inescapably part of the duties of women. The real reason for the fewer numbers of women leaders within trade unions seems to be in the one sentence the author does not elaborate upon — "it is also true that no trade union organization has seriously and in an organised manner taken up the job of preparing a cadre of women leaders..."

Vimal Ranadive of the CITU sees the lack of conscious and persistent effort of trade unions to organise women around equal wages, maternity benefits and retrenchment as the main reason for their low membership. She notes that in many instances the leadership of trade unions has gone to the extent of discouraging women from coming forward to be on executive committees and the like.[8] She suggests therefore that a committee of women trade unionists be formed in each industry under the guidance of their respective unions. Another study notes that not one trade union is known to have prosecuted a factory owner for ignoring the health problems his factory causes to his female employees.[9]

Perception of Patriarchy

None of these unions consider with any seriousness the hold of patriarchal ideology over the working class or over the trade union leadership itself. In their weekly journals, workers are always referred to as workmen and in the masculine pronoun. There is occasional mention in these journals, of women workers who have played heroic roles in strikes. However, since such reports are few, they tend rather to reinforce the impression that women rarely participate in union activities so that when they do, it rates a special mention. There are instances such as the fight of women workers of Ritz Continental Hotel, Calcutta, who had been retrenched in 1976,[10] a demonstration by working and middle class women at Vishakapatnam before the

Collector's office demanding restoration of the rice quota and reduction in its price in January 1975,[11] and the arrest of some women belonging to the families of the workers of a textile mill in Indore who had been agitating for the opening of the mill.[12] Apart from isolated instances like this, however, where women alone have agitated, it would appear from reading the journals of the trade unions that the general workforce is composed entirely of men. The last instance does not even refer to women workers, but to the families of workmen. In fact, there tends to be a general emphasis on such women outside the workforce as forming a reserve force of trade unions. The railway strike of 1974, the movement for democratic rights in Durgapur and the strike of South Eastern Railway workers in 1970, and many other struggles of workers have witnessed the active involvement of women of the striking workers' families in organising pickets, taking part in demonstrations, facing police attacks and so on.

However, it is precisely because these women are playing their roles within the established familial structure that trade unions find it easier to recognize their participation. Without in any way reducing the importance of the part these women play in workers' struggles, it is necessary to recognize that they are not stepping out of limits of their positions as dependent daughters and wives of workers. The importance of distinguishing between the role of women outside the workforce and of women as workers becomes clear when we consider the kind of conclusions that can be drawn from over-emphasizing the significance of the former. It becomes possible to argue that for family reasons women can be relied on as a reserve force of trade unions and that their participation through the family unit as wives, sisters and mothers of workers is an important structural basis of understanding women's role in trade unions.[13] To view the participation of women in trade union activity primarily in terms of a reserve force functioning in the family structure obscures the oppressive forces operating within that structure. It also prevents an examination of how far women workers are restricted from functioning on an equal footing with their male counterparts within trade unions.

INTUC's perception of women is along the paternalistic traditional lines of Gandhism. The education of women is seen as necessary so that families are better looked after and high efficiency maintained among workers. Women are seen as excelling in certain spheres such as nursing, mid-wifery, teaching in elementary schools and the fine arts. The vice-president of INTUC in a speech to the Rajya Sabha suggested that in the International Women's Year certain specific occupations should be reserved for women. These occupations were teaching, nursing and social service. Other articles in *Indian Worker* reflected the understanding that housework is a woman's responsibility and so solutions are sought in terms of lightening her load through labour-saving devices and reduction in working hours so that women can attend to their homes. The gentleness of women is expected to help the trade union movement become tolerant, patient and non-violent.[14]

Since the understanding of women of AITUC and CITU is set within the framework of the class struggle, their perception is less paternalistic than that of the INTUC. A resolution passed by AITUC at its 32nd session in 1983 noted, "Feudal and semi-feudal attitudes to women are widespread which also results in a lack of seriousness in the matter of taking up the special problems of women workers or in involving them in trade union activities." Earlier at the 31st session the AITUC, while calling on women workers to come forward and join trade unions, also called upon the unions to help women shoulder more responsibilities in their respective unions.

Resolutions of Unions

In 1979 the CITU held a national convention of working women. The report of this convention noted that even in industries and occupations in which women were a sizeable group, they were not represented in the leading bodies of the union. This was attributed not to any natural disinclination on their part, but to social attitudes which restricted the role of women.[15] Particularly after the declaration of 1975 as International Women's Year, all three unions have been holding conventions on working women in different parts of the country and passing resolutions on different aspects of women's employment. A specimen resolution from each union is given below:

(a)   AITUC in 1980 at its 31st session demanded special machinery to implement the Equal Remuneration Act ensuring the security of employment of women in industries where they are already employed, eradication of discriminatory practices in regard to employment of women, improvement in women's skills and protection from harassment particularly at their places of work.

(b)   The working committee of the INTUC submitted a memorandum on various issues concerning labour and national economy to the Union Finance Minister in 1980. This memorandum had a note on women workers, pointing to the falling rate of women's employment in industries and demanding more employment opportunities for women, facilities for pre-employment training in selected industries and services, and creches, day-care institutions and working women's hostels.

The INTUC has a women's wing, whose activities from 1971 to 1984 according to the reports of the sessions, have been mainly the organisation of seminars, conferences and educational and training programmes, and participation in the Indian Committee for the 'celebration' of International Women's Year.

(c)   The CITU at its working committee meeting in December 1975 adopted a resolution criticising the Ordinance on Equal Pay for Equal Work as inadequate in terms of implementation and demanding the protection of women workers from the threat of retrenchment following its introduction.

While resolutions have been passed and convocations and seminars held, there is no evidence of a single strike or agitation which was called on the issues of equal wages or the non-provision of maternity benefits and child care facilities or the retrenchment of women workers in the wake of the Equal Remuneration Act. Nor is there any discussion at all about the exploitative sexual division of labour in the home - women's 'household responsibilities' are often cited as a reason for low trade union participation but never questioned.

The issue of equal pay for equal work is one which best reflects the position of women within the trade union movement and is worth considering in some detail.

The Issue of Equal Remuneration for Equal Work

India ratified the ILO Convention on Equal Pay in 1958 but the Equal Remuneration Ordinance was promulgated only in 1975. This was ratified later by Parliament and the Equal Remuneration Act was passed in 1976. The provisions of this Act were: (i) men and women workers doing the same work or work of a similar nature must be equally paid. "Same work or work of a similar nature" was defined as "work in respect of which the skill, effort and responsibility required are the same when performed under similar working conditions by a man or woman...". (ii) There was to be no discrimination against women at the time of recruitment. (iii) Employers defaulting were to be punished by a fine of upto Rs. 5000/- but there was no provision for imprisonment.

However, there was no automatic introduction of equal pay for equal work; the industries concerned would be notified by the government within a period of three years. This would give employers ample time to reorganise their workforce in such a manner that jobs classified on the basis of sex would be reclassified in terms of higher and lower categories. Also, the term 'same work or work of a similar nature' is capable of providing loopholes because women's employment is generally restricted to a few spheres where men do not work. Hence the demand in USA for equal pay for "comparable" work, that is, comparable in terms of its value for the employer as well as in terms of the skill required to perform it seems much more in true with reality. The Act moreover, did not ban retrenchment of women workers and thus large numbers of women did in fact, lose their jobs in the wake of the Act.

All three trade unions being studied have responded very favourably to the Act in terms of passing resolutions and drawing the attention of the government to lapses in complying with the Act. The General Secretary of the Indian National Rural Labour Federation who was also Vice President of INTUC wrote to the Chief Ministers of five states in 1975 drawing their attention to the discriminatory provisions in the wages fixed by them for female workers in rural areas. If the disparity was not removed the INRLF would be 'constrained to launch an agitation', the General Secretary cautioned.[16] However, there is no information in subsequent issues of *Indian Worker* about the response of the concerned Chief Ministers and whether the disparity was indeed rectified. At any rate, no agitation was launched on the issue.

The President of the Tamil Nadu INTUC in a statement to the Press decried the action of plantation owners, reducing men's wages to those of women in the wake of the Act.[17] INTUC therefore appealed to the Tamil Nadu Government to see that the spirit of the Act was not violated.

The AITUC, at its 30th session in 1976 welcomed the Act but

drew attention to the distortions in its implementation. "In the tea plantations... in the name of implementing the Act managements have been depriving women workers of their real wages or increasing their workload. Similar instances have been noted in the construction industry, where .... the employers have even resorted to retrenchment of women workers .... to evade implementation of the Act. The government has also not implemented the requirements of setting up the implementation machinery and advisory committees enjoined by the Act ..." The AITUC demanded that these aspects be looked into and rectified.

In December 1975 the CITU working committee demanded further amendments to the ordinance — (a) a ban on retrenchment of women workers with effect from the date of its promulgation and immediate implementation of the ordinance without the grace period of three years, (b) heavier punishments for lapses in complying with its provisions, (c) withdrawal of the power of the government to declare unequal wages in certain occupations and (d) the implementation of the Ordinance to be supervised by a Committee consisting of elected trade union representatives not those nominated by government.[18] In 1976, the CITU unions in the plantations of Karnataka refused to sign an agreement with the management which replaced the words 'men' and 'women' by 'Grade I' and 'Grade II'. By this agreement Grade I wages would be paid to men and Grade II to women. A memorandum protesting against this manoeuvre was sent to the Karnataka Government and Union Labour Minister by the Karnataka Provincial Plantation Workers' Union.

These are only a few major examples of resolutions and memoranda, but the fact remains that there have been very few cases of complaints filed under the Equal Remuneration Act.[19] This is due to various factors — the greater vulnerability of women workers which makes them more cautious, and the lack of publicity given to the Act among women workers. Trade Unions have evidently not considered the issue of equal pay important enough to be taken up seriously. A report in the Financial Express at the time of the Ordinance said "In the present state of stabilised relationship between unions and managements in plantations the unions are able to perceive and privately admit that but for some marginal exceptions, the nature of male, female and child employment in plantations is essentially based on occupational work logic and not sex discrimination, but are unwilling to take a public posture on this Act for fear they may appear as pro-management"[20]

This report was unsubstantiated by interviews or names of specific unions, but its credibility bears up to scrutiny when one considers the actual actions taken by the trade unions to enforce the Act. As has been noted earlier, there has not been a single agitation or strike on the issue, although the Act continues it be more infringed than adhered to.

The picture that emerges is one in which trade unions would appear to be as embedded in patriarchal ideology as other organisations. I would like to make the point here that there is a qualitative difference in the perception of the INTUC and CITU. It is not my intention to obscure the differences in the views represented by them on oppression of women. AITUC and CITU, viewing society in terms of class struggle, regard the prevailing attitudes on women as remnants of feudal ideology, whereas INTUC is able to do little more than state pious intentions while continuing to view women in the framework of traditional Indian wife and mother.

Moreover, it is of vital importance to see that there are powerful movements within trade unions of the left to pressurise the leadership to take up the specific nature of female workers' oppression. There are women's caucuses within CITU and AITUC which have made special efforts in the last two to three years to recruit women, and have drawn up a charter of demands of women employees.[21] 'CITU's journal on women workers, *Voice of the Working Women* was started in 1980. The issues spanning the last five years have recorded a tremendous volume of struggle by women all over the country—peasants fighting against harassment by landlords, factory workers demanding better working conditions, middle class professional working women striking for higher salaries and better conditions of living, air-hostesses against discriminatory terms of employment. In the same period, CITU's official journal *Working Class* reflects none of this powerful political activity, so that in effect *Working Class* is the journal of CITU's main members and *Voice* of the female. The very founding of the journal however, points to the burgeoning consciousness within trade unions of the left that class and gender oppression feed on each other and must be fought simultaneously.

REFERENCES

1.   Figures compiled by the Ministry of Labour, quoted in *Indian Worker,* January 8, 1979, vol. XXVII, no. 14.

2.   Mathur and Mathur, *Trade Union Movement in India.* Chaitanya Publishing House, Allahabad, 1962, p. 71.

3.   *Socio-economic conditions of women workers in Mines,* Labour Bureau, Government of India, 1979.

4.   Jhabvala, Renana, *Closing Doors,* Setu Publishers, Ahmedabad, 1982, cited by Neerja Chowdhury, 'First Victims of Mechanisations'; Statesman, November 25, 1985.

5.   *'Women Workers in Organised and Unorganised Sectors in India',* in *Indian Worker,* March 9, 1981 Vol. XXIV, no. 23.

6.   Mathur and Mathur, op.cit., p. 72.

7.   Dixit, J.C., *Indian Worker,* Anniversary Number, May 5, 1975.

8.   Ranadive, Vimal, *Fight Unitedly for the cause of Indian Working Women,* CITU, 1980, pp. 65-6.

9.   Anklesaria, Shehnaaz, *Factories Ignore Workers' Health,* in *The Statesman,* July 2, 1984.

10. *Working Class,* Vol. 5, No. 7, March, 1976.

11. *Trade Union Record,* January 9, 1975, Vol. XXXII, No. 1.

12. *Indian Worker,* June 6, 1977, Vol. XXV, No. 36.

13. Chaudhari, Maitrayee, *Participation of Women in the Indian Trade Union Movement* (unpublished), M. Phil. Dissertation, JNU, Delhi, 1951.

14. A representative selection of articles from *Indian Worker.* Dewan, Subhash Chander, *"Modern Education and Gandhiji",* Gandhi Jayanti Number, 1977; Dhabe, S. W., *"Women's Emancipation",* September 30, 1974, Vol. XXIII; Srinivasan, V., *"The Emancipation of Working Women",* February 21, 1977. Vol. XXV, No. 21; Ghiya, D.P., *"Work Among Women",* Gandhi Jayanti Number 1970; Ramanujan, G., *"Women's Healing Touch",* February 16, 1981, Vol. XXVIII, No. 31.

15. Ranadive, Vimal, op. cit pp 33.

16. *Indian Worker,* May 19, 1975, Vol. XXIII, No. 32.

17. *Indian Worker,* November 15, 1976, Vol. XXV, No. 7.

18. *Working Class,* Vol. 5, No. 4, December. 1975.

19. Jaising, Indira, *"Evolution of Changes in the Law Relating to Women during the decade 1975-84",* on behalf of the Lawyers Collective: Paper presented at the National Seminar on 'A Decade on Women's Movement in India', SNDT Women's University, Bombay, January, 1985.

20. *'Equal Remuneration Ordinance"* Financial Express 'February 1, 1976.

21. Patel, Vibhuti, *Women's Liberation in India,* New Left Review, 153, September-October, 1985.

Notes on Contributors

Aleyamma Vijayan is associated with the life and struggles of the fisherfolk of Kerala since 1978. She is presently working with the Programme for Community Organisation, Thiruvananthapuram.

Nivedita Menon teaches in Lady Shri Ram College, Delhi and is actively interested in the politics of gender.

P M Mathew is the Director of Institute of Small Enterprises and Development, Cochin. He has extensively written on women's issues. His current research interests are in areas like planning, organisation of the unorganised sector and development problems in the special context of industrialisation.

Priya is an active member of Pennurimai·Iyakkam, a women's group in Madras active among mainly poor women in the slums of Madras city.

Radha Kumar has been active in the women's movement since mid-1970s. She has also written extensively on the women's movement.

Renana Jhabvala is Secretary of SEWA and in-charge of the Economic Wing of SEWA and of union activities. She was awarded the Padmashree in 1990. Her publications cover a range of issues - - girl students, women workers in textiles, beedi-rolling, etc. Her experience is varied. She was the Director of Andhra Bank,

a member of the Labour Welfare Board, and is a trustee of
Ahmedabad Women's Action Group.

Rohini Gavankar was the Dean of the faculty of Social Sciences in
SNDT Women's University. She is a member of the Advisory
Committee on Women's Studies, SNDT University. She is the
editor of the Newsletter of the Indian Association for Women's
Studies. Her published articles cover industrial women workers,
women in Panchayat Raj, women's political participation.

V Rukmini Rao has been active in the women's movement since the
mid-seventies. She has worked as an Associate Fellow at the
National Labour Institute and Public Enterprises Centre for
Continuing Education, New Delhi. She is a member of the Saheli
Collective, New Delhi. She has done research on problems
relating to women's work and the division of labour in industry.
She is currently working as a consultant to the Norwegian
Development Agency and is involved with education and
development of rural women in Andhra Pradesh.

Sahba Husain has been involved in research in gender studies. Her
focus has been largely on women's employment in the
unorganised sector, the self-perception of women, the question
of organisation and women's participation in struggles. She has
worked at the Centre for Women's Development Studies and at
the Women's Development Centre, Indraprastha College, Delhi.
She is actively involved with the women's movement. She has
recently started working in the area of religion, identity and
women's consciousness.

Saswati Ghosh teaches Economics in City College, University of
Calcutta. She is involved with the women's movement in
Calcutta. She regularly writes for the local newspapers and
periodicals. She is now working on women's work and
discrimination.

Shaswati Mazumdar teaches German at the Department of Modern
European Languages, University of Delhi. She was Joint
Secretary of the Delhi University Teachers' Association (DUTA)
from September 1985 to October 1987, a period which
encompassed both the strikes referred to in her articles.

Sujata Gothoskar has been active in the union movement and the women's movement in Bombay from the mid-1970s. She is active in the Union Research Group, Workers' Solidarity Centre and the Forum Against Oppression of Women. Her articles, reports and books deal with issues like women workers, union strategies, occupational health problems of women workers and struggles and organisations of women.

V. Vasanthi Devi is Professor of history and the Principal of the Government College for Women, Kumbakoram, Tamil Nadu. She has been active in the women's movement and has organised women students and teachers on women's issues. She was the Joint Secretary of the Tamil Nadu Government Collegiate Teachers' Association. She is the President of a women's study centre - 'Penn' (woman). She is now working on the issue of dowry and female infanticide in Usilampatti taluka in Tamil Nadu.

Index